THE ART OF WOODWORKING

TABLES AND DESKS

THE ART OF WOODWORKING

TABLES AND DESKS

TIME-LIFE BOOKS
ALEXANDRIA, VIRGINIA

ST. REMY PRESS
MONTREAL • NEW YORK

THE ART OF WOODWORKING was produced by
ST. REMY PRESS

PUBLISHER	Kenneth Winchester
PRESIDENT	Pierre Léveillé
Series Editor	Pierre Home-Douglas
Series Art Director	Francine Lemieux
Senior Editors	Marc Cassini (Text)
	Heather Mills (Research)
Art Directors	Normand Boudreault, Luc Germain,
	Solange Laberge
Designers	Lina Desrochers, Hélène Dion,
	Jean-Guy Doiron, Michel Giguère
Research Editor	Jim McRae
Picture Editor	Christopher Jackson
Writers	Andrew Jones, Rob Lutes
Research Assistant	Bryan Quinn
Contributing Illustrators	Gilles Beauchemin, Roland Bergerat,
	Michel Blais, Jean-Pierre Bourgeois,
	Ronald Durepos, Jacques Perrault,
	James Thérien
Administrator	Natalie Watanabe
Production Manager	Michelle Turbide
System Coordinator	Jean-Luc Roy
Photographers	Robert Chartier, Christian Levesque
Administrative Assistant	Dominique Gagné
Proofreader	Judith Yelon
Indexer	Christine M. Jacobs

Time-Life Books is a division of Time Life Inc.,
a wholly owned subsidiary of
THE TIME INC. BOOK COMPANY

TIME LIFE INC.

President and CEO	John M. Fahey
Editor-in-chief	John L. Papanek

TIME-LIFE BOOKS

President	John D. Hall
Vice-President, Director of Marketing	Nancy K. Jones
Executive Editor	Roberta Conlan
Executive Art Director	Ellen Robling
Consulting Editor	John R. Sullivan
Production Manager	Marlene Zack

THE CONSULTANTS

Jon Arno is a consultant, cabinetmaker, and freelance writer who lives in Troy, Michigan. He also conducts seminars on wood identification and early American furniture design.

Kam Ghaffari is a freelance writer and editor. He has his own business in Rhode Island designing and building one-of-a-kind and limited production furniture. Kam's background also includes working professionally in furniture reproduction and fine carpentry and studying with furniture patriarchs Wendell Castle of the U.S. and England's Fred Baier.

Giles Miller-Mead taught advanced cabinetmaking at Montreal technical schools for more than ten years. A native of New Zealand, he has worked as a restorer of antique furniture.

Tables & Desks
   p. cm.—(The Art of woodworking)
Includes index.
ISBN 0-8094-9512-0
1. Tables 2. Desks 3. Furniture making I. Time-Life Books.
II. Title: Tables and desks. III. Series.
TT197.5.T3T33 1994
684.1'3—dc20   93-49732
                                                    CIP

For information about any Time-Life book,
please call 1-800-621-7026, or write:
Reader Information
Time-Life Customer Service
P.O. Box C-32068
Richmond, Virginia
23261-2068

CONTENTS

Simon Watts talks about

HIS RECYCLED DESK

I have worked with wood for a half-century, building furniture, houses, and small boats and still I marvel at the endless possibilities of the material. However, as I get older and the trees get fewer, I prefer to use wood that has already had a career as a bridge, a boat, or a building—two careers, if you count being a tree as the first.

Far from a limitation, I've found that working with recycled wood stretches the imagination and takes considerable ingenuity. Used boat lumber is the greatest challenge because it is curved and full of closely spaced fastenings.

I made the desk in the photo for my San Francisco apartment using Douglas-fir reclaimed from a local wrecking yard. After removing all visible fastenings, I wire-brushed the surfaces and ran the boards though a thickness planer. I made no attempt to conceal bolt holes, iron stains, and other evidence of the timber's previous life; instead, I incorporated them into the desk.

Like most of the larger pieces I make now, this one knocks down completely. The four boards of the top are doweled together without glue and the supporting structure consists of mortise-and-tenon joints and draw pins. Driving the tapered pegs home pulls the joint together. The stretcher is tenoned through the legs and secured with loose wedges.

Unless you have delusions of grandeur, there is no point in making a working surface larger than you can comfortably reach when sitting down. That means a maximum of 6 feet long and no more than half that in depth—the size of this desk.

I prefer to keep only the items I associate with desks in the drawers: writing materials, stamps, paper clips, stapler, and so on. Computers, monitors, printers, and associated equipment are, I think, much better housed in a separate unit. I don't like file storage built into a desk: Drawers full of files make a piece of furniture monumental, even intimidating, in appearance. Also, a person's filing needs change, so I think it is better to add or change file units than to remodel or replace a desk.

It may happen that this desk will outlive its usefulness and the wood again turned into something else. With no glued joints and no hidden fastenings, that would be easy—and perhaps suitable considering the recycled nature of the piece. The desk will be my gift to a woodworker in the next century.

Simon Watts is a woodworker, writer, and teacher. He now lives in San Francisco where he offers nationally recognized classes in wooden boat building. He is also the West Coast editor for American Woodworker magazine and last year published three boat-building manuals.

Kam Ghaffari discusses

DESIGNING TABLES

I have built practically every type of furniture, from decorative high-style chairs to kitchen cabinets, but I'm fascinated by tables. Both the first piece of furniture I made and the first one I designed were tables. It's an undeniable challenge to create a beautiful chair that is also comfortable, or an elegant entertainment center designed specifically around the sizes and functions of its contents. But for sheer simplicity and design freedom, you can't beat a table.

Sooner or later, many woodworkers want to start designing their own furniture. It's something I strongly encourage; designing greatly increases the satisfaction derived from woodworking. A table is a great place to start. A table has relatively few structural elements and technical requirements: If you've got a flat top and a solid support system to hold it up, you have got a functional table. The rest is up to you. Take into account strength requirements, use, and size when planning the piece. Will this be a heavy-duty kid-proof kitchen table or a delicate decorative hall table, for example? Then bring in forms and shapes that please you. Subtle points such as a delicately shaped leg, decorative joinery, a clever handmade mechanism, or a particularly handsome piece of wood can be showcased in a table.

Your piece can be simple or complex, as austere as Shaker or as ostentatious as rococo, based on designs of the 1930s or the 1730s—or something unique and imaginative. Its design can also address a particular need not met by commercially available furniture, like a telephone table, or a backgammon or chess table.

The table in the photo was influenced by the classic Danish designs of Hans Wegner, as well as by my appreciation of the aspen leaf, hence the name, Aspen Table. This was designed for streamlined production without sacrificing its handcrafted look. I wanted a table that knocked down flat for shipping, yet was sturdy when assembled. A light-duty, three-legged table is stable if the legs are evenly spaced and far enough apart. It also doesn't require leveling on uneven floors.

I tenoned the turned legs into the shaped rails, then devised a removable grooved metal plate that, with screws going into threaded inserts in the rails, ties them all together. The rails are also countersunk for screws that fit into threaded inserts in the stable multi-ply top. The inlays in the tops are routed with a collar riding in a female template. The ivory-colored material is tinted patching resin for solid-surface countertops. The green aluminum veins are computer milled to ensure a precise fit time after time. For a single inlay, this part could be cut with a jeweler's saw and file.

Kam Ghaffari designs, builds, and writes about furniture at his studio in Westerly, Rhode Island.

Tony Searer on

A SPANISH-STYLE DESK

When you run a commercial furniture shop, creating a unique and pleasing design can be an invigorating challenge. Foremost in the process is listening to the customer and balancing practical and esthetic considerations.

The buyers of the desk in the photo wanted a handsome sculptural piece of furniture that would also allow them to display art objects. Other design considerations involved incorporating three hanging file drawers as well as numerous small drawers and cubbies with a self-contained light source.

The drop-front design was inspired by the original *vargueño* traveling desks brought from old Spain to the frontier of New Mexico. The carved motifs and turned legs are derived from pieces that survived from the Spanish Colonial era. The entire piece is made from sugar pine, a wood native to the western United States.

There is an enduring and rich tradition of carving and furniture making in northern New Mexico. Ramon Martinez, sitting at the desk, exemplifies this centuries-old Hispanic tradition. Thirty years with the company, most as a shop foreman, have shaped him into a true master craftsman. In building this piece, Ramon made the desk as authentic as possible within the context of the design. All the primary joints are mortise-and-tenon, which is historically appropriate. The raised panels float for expansion and the decorative hardware is hand-forged. The desk features an inset leather desk pad. The knobs on the outside are connected to concealed bolts that hold the leather pad in place. The bolts can be released so the leather surface can be easily replaced.

The end result is a compact and functional desk that adds a very warm and pleasing design element to the user's home. The desk has been in use for some years now and the antiqued finish we applied—a combination of various hand-rubbed oils and sprayed lacquers—has only improved with age.

Tony Searer owns Southwest Spanish Craftsmen, a furniture shop in Sante Fe, New Mexico, that specializes in Spanish Colonial, Spanish Provincial, and its own classic southwestern styles. Previously, he designed and built exhibits for the Museum of New Mexico.

TABLE AND DESK BASICS

Lumber quality varies widely, even within the same grade. Taking the time to examine and select boards carefully at a lumberyard will help you obtain the best stock for your project.

Although the following chapters of this book focus on the nuts and bolts of table and desk construction, there is more to building a piece of furniture than cutting joints and assembling components. Before any of this can happen, some time must be spent designing the piece, and selecting and preparing the lumber. This chapter focuses on the skills you will need to carry out these preparatory steps. For some craftsmen, the preliminaries are among the most enjoyable aspects of a project. Hand-picking a mahogany board at the lumberyard, or unwrapping a package of exotic wood from a mail-order supplier, for example, can be rewarding experiences.

First, you need to select the kind of table or desk that suits your needs. The illustrated gallery of table and desk styles beginning on page 22 can provide a starting point in your search for a suitable design. The dimensions you incorporate will affect both the appearance and suitability of the piece. Standard dimensions are discussed in detail on page 21.

Once you have selected a design (or sketched one yourself), it is time to buy the lumber. The sections on wood movement *(page 14)*, ordering wood *(page 16)*, and deriving a cutting list from a sketch *(page 17)* provide the basic information you will need to purchase the wood for your project.

With your stock in hand, one crucial step remains before you can start to put your work together: preparing the stock *(page 19)*. This process includes jointing and planing rough wood so it is smooth and square, and cutting stock to length and width. For rough, unsurfaced lumber, first pass one face across the jointer, then one edge, producing two surfaces at 90° to each other. Next, plane the other face of the board to make it parallel to the first. When the stock is square and smooth, you are ready to rip it to width and crosscut it to length. If you buy S2S stock, which already has both faces surfaced, pass one edge across the jointer, then rip and crosscut it to size. S4S stock, which has all its surfaces prepared, can be ripped and crosscut immediately. Only edges that will be joined together, such as boards being edge-glued to make a tabletop, need to be jointed.

Finally, remember that it is important to tackle your project methodically. For greatest efficiency, lay out your tools in the shop so that your wood follows a relatively direct route from rough stock to final assembly. When you have jointed your stock and cut it to size, fashion your joints and sand all components before assembly.

An orbital sander smoothes the top of a double-pedestal desk. After a final pass with a fine-grit paper, the desk will be ready for a finish.

WOOD MOVEMENT

Wood gains and loses moisture as the relative humidity of the surrounding air changes. And as the wood's moisture content changes, so do its dimensions and weight. These changes can cause problems for a piece of furniture, some merely irritating, others much more serious. Knowing how moisture affects wood and making the appropriate allowances will help you avoid difficulty.

The water contained in a piece of wood is measured as a percentage of the wood's oven-dry, or water-free weight. For example, if a 50-pound piece of wood weighs 40 pounds when it is oven-dry, the weight of the shed water—10 pounds—divided by the wood's dry weight—40 pounds—is the moisture content of the original piece: in this case, 25 percent.

Wood contains water in two ways: as free water in its cell cavities and as bound water in its cell walls. When wood is cut and exposed to the air, it sheds its free water first. When all free water is expelled, the wood is said to be at its fiber saturation point (FSP), which is typically between 23 and 30 percent moisture content. Up to this point, as shown in the illustration at right, there has been no change in the dimensions of the piece; it simply weighs less. As wood dries further, however, water is removed from the cell walls, and the board shrinks.

Under normal circumstances, wood never regains its free water, but changes in humidity in the air do affect the amount of moisture in the cell walls. At 100 percent relative humidity, wood reaches its FSP, holding as much bound water as possible. At 0 percent humidity, wood is devoid of all moisture. Usually, because the water content of wood reflects the moisture present in the atmosphere, the moisture content of most woods ranges between 5 and 20 percent. The fluctuation in relative humidity of nearly 80 percent between typical North American winters and summers can cause substantial wood movement over the course of a year. Because of their size, tabletops and desktops are especially prone to movement. A 3-foot-wide top with the wood grain running along its length can experience annual movement of more than 1 inch across its width. This can cause serious difficulties for an extension table, for example, which relies on the perfect alignment of various components.

You can do several things to compensate for the effects of humidity changes on wood. In your shop, use a humidifier in winter and a dehumidifier in summer to keep the humidity level as constant as possible. Also, make allowances for wood movement in the construction of your work. With an extension table (page 90), for example, orient the wood grain of the top to run across the width of the table, not along its length. This way, wood movement will not affect alignment of the pieces. The method you use to attach a top is equally important. Several effective methods are shown starting on page 96. Using frame-and-panel construction (page 31) for the casework of a desk will allow wood to expand and contract without affecting the stability of the piece. Some woods tend to swell and shrink more than others. Your lumber dealer can help you select dimensionally stable species for your projects.

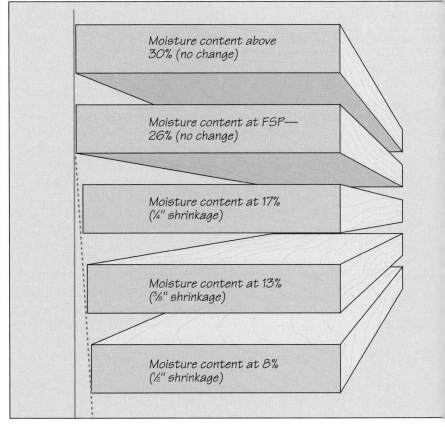

Moisture content above 30% (no change)

Moisture content at FSP— 26% (no change)

Moisture content at 17% (¼" shrinkage)

Moisture content at 13% (⅜" shrinkage)

Moisture content at 8% (½" shrinkage)

When the moisture content of a 2-by-10 plain-sawn plank of softwood lumber drops below its fiber saturation point (FSP), the wood shrinks. At 17 percent, the board is ¼ inch narrower than it was at its FSP; it loses another ¼ inch of width when kiln-dried to 8 percent. Shrinkage depends partly on the density of the wood; generally, a denser species shrinks and swells more than a less dense one.

WOOD SHRINKAGE

Tangential and radial shrinkage

Wood does not shrink uniformly. As shown by the the dotted lines in the illustration at right, tangential shrinkage—roughly parallel to the growth rings—is about twice the radial shrinkage, which occurs across the rings. This difference causes boards and panels to warp when they shrink or swell as relative humidity changes. Shrinkage along the length of a board is usually insignificant. A 2-by-10 plank, for example, which shrinks ½ inch across its width might lose less than ¹⁄₁₆ inch along an 8-foot length. When building tops for tables and desks, orient the grain in the direction that will cause the fewest problems. Quartersawn stock, which has growth rings that are at right angles to the face, has less of a tendency to cup and is a good choice for tops.

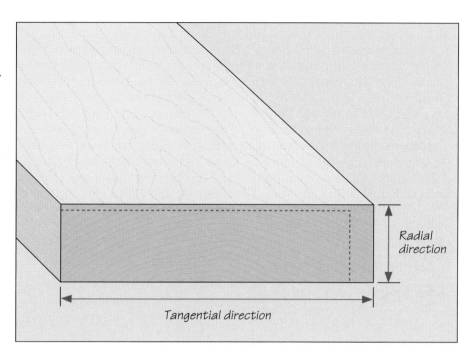

Radial direction

Tangential direction

WOOD GRAIN AND JOINERY

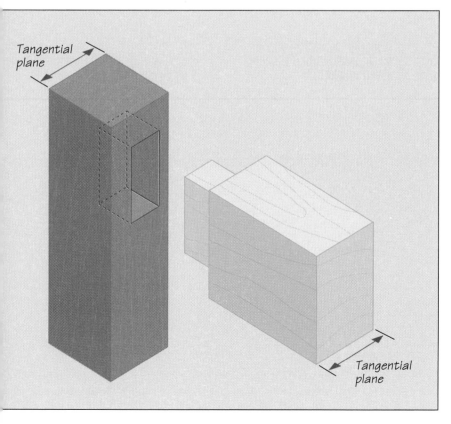

Tangential plane

Tangential plane

Optimizing grain direction

Wood movement can have an effect on the strength of a joint. Orient the grain of the mating pieces of a joint so they will move in the same direction. In the mortise-and-tenon joint shown at left, the boards' tangential planes are parallel to each other. Consequently, the wood movement that one piece experiences will be closely matched by the other and the joint will not be weakened. Assembling a joint with the tangential planes of the two pieces at right angles could weaken the joint or even force it apart.

SELECTING AND ORDERING WOOD

Lumber for your table or desk project can come from several sources, each with its own advantages and drawbacks. The local lumberyard is the most obvious supplier, and often the most convenient, but the selection may be limited to construction woods such as pine, spruce, and other softwoods. Though you may find the occasional cache of hardwood, more often than not you will have to venture farther afield, consulting the Yellow Pages or woodworking magazines to find dealers who specialize in some of the less common hardwoods used for fine furniture. You will usually pay more, but the quality of the wood should be higher too.

There are other less costly options for finding the wood you need. A lumber mill may sell you boards at a reasonable price, but the wood will most often need to be seasoned and surfaced, which means that you must own a jointer and planer. Also, larger mills are often reluctant to fill small orders. Recycled boards are becoming increasingly popular with woodworkers, a result of the scarcity of certain woods. Salvaged wood is relatively inexpensive and, because it often comes from old-growth timber, it can be visually and structurally superior to recently harvested lumber. Regardless of your chosen supply, define your needs carefully before ordering wood. The tips that follow will help you get what you need at a reasonable cost. Being well prepared will also speed the process considerably.

• **Species:** Ask for the specific wood species, rather than a broad family name. For example, order Western red cedar, not simply cedar. To be sure you get what

CALCULATING BOARD FEET

Ordering lumber by the board foot

The "board foot" is a unit of measurement used to calculate the volume of a given amount of stock. It is commonly used with hardwood lumber. As shown in the illustration at right, the standard board foot is equivalent to a piece that is 1 inch thick, 12 inches wide, and 12 inches long. To calculate the number of board feet in a piece of wood, multiply its three dimensions together. Then, divide the result by 144 if the dimensions are in inches, or by 12 if just one dimension is in feet.

The formula for a standard board:
1" x 12" x 12" ÷ 144 = 1
(or 1" x 12" x 1' ÷ 12 = 1)
So if you had a 6-foot-long plank that is 1 inch thick and 4 inches wide, you would calculate the board feet as follows: 1" x 4" x 6' ÷ 12 = 2 (or 2 board feet). Other examples are shown in the illustration. Remember that board feet are calculated on the basis of the nominal rather than actual dimensions of the stock; consequently, the board feet contained in a 2-by-4 that actually measures 1½-by-3½ inches would be calculated using the larger dimensions.

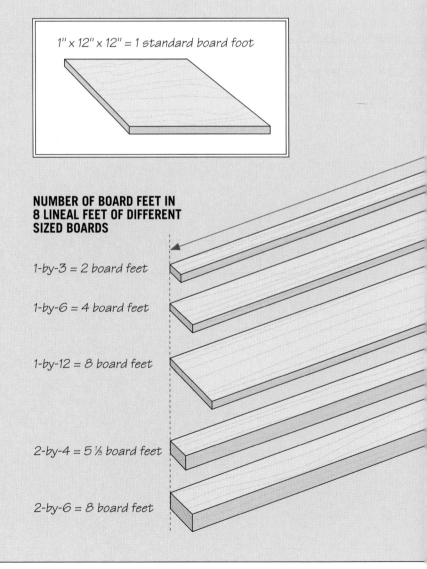

1" x 12" x 12" = 1 standard board foot

NUMBER OF BOARD FEET IN 8 LINEAL FEET OF DIFFERENT SIZED BOARDS

1-by-3 = 2 board feet

1-by-6 = 4 board feet

1-by-12 = 8 board feet

2-by-4 = 5⅓ board feet

2-by-6 = 8 board feet

ou want, learn the botanical name of ne wood you want and ask for it.

• **Quantity:** When ordering wood, pecify whether you want the stock in oard feet or lineal feet. A lineal foot s merely an expression of a board's ength, regardless of its width or thickess. The board foot is a specific volume f wood; it is usually necessary for orderng hardwoods, which are often available n random widths only. See page 16 for nformation about calculating board feet.

• **Size:** Wood is sold in nominal rather han real sizes, so make allowances for

the difference when ordering surfaced lumber. A 2-by-4 is actually 1½"-by-3½". The thickness of hardwoods is often expressed as an improper fraction in quarters of an inch. A 1½-inch-thick hardwood board, for example, is expressed as 6⁄4. The nominal and real dimensions of unsurfaced, green boards are the same.

• **Grade:** Within the higher hardwood grades, the primary difference between the various grades is appearance rather than strength. Considering the difference in price, it is best to reserve the best stock for the visible parts of your projects, using less expensive, lower-grade wood for hidden components. Consult

your lumber dealer for a chart of the different grades available.

• **Seasoning:** Lumber is sold either kiln dried (KD), air dried (AD), or green. Kiln-dried wood is generally the most stable. It has a moisture content (MC) of 8 percent, whereas air-dried wood has a MC of 12 to 20 percent. Air-dried wood is often preferred by carvers.

• **Surfacing:** Surfacing refers to how the stock is prepared at the mill before it comes to the lumberyard. Softwood lumber is usually surfaced on both faces; hardwood is often sold rough. If you have a planer and jointer, buying rough lumber and surfacing it yourself will prove less expensive.

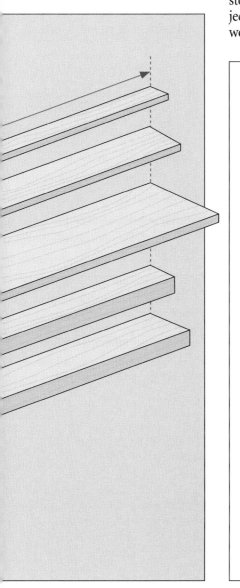

A CUTTING LIST

Making and using a cutting list
A cutting list records the finished sizes of lumber needed for a particular piece of furniture. If one is not included with the plans you purchase, you will have to make your own based on a sketch of the design. Use the formula shown on page 16 to total the number of board feet for each component of the project; add 20 to 40 percent (depending on the grade) to account for waste and defects in the wood. Also use the nominal thickness (indicated in parentheses) of the pieces in your calculations. For the simple table shown at right, which totals 25¼ board feet, you should purchase 30 to 35 board feet of lumber. Assign each component a letter for later reference.

CUTTING LIST

PIECE	QTY	TH.	W.	L.	MATERIAL	BOARD FEET
A Top	1	¾ (1")	36"	60"	ash	15
B Side rails	2	¾ (1")	4"	48½"	ash	2.7
C End rails	2	¾ (1")	4"	26½"	ash	1.5
D Legs	4	2½ (3")	2½"	29"	ash	6.0

LUMBER DEFECTS

Lumber defects are flaws that reduce a board's strength or workability, or adversely affect its appearance. They can result from the way the lumber is prepared at the mill, the methods of seasoning and storing, or, more often than not, the natural growing conditions experienced by the tree.

Not all defects are unwelcome. Some natural imperfections can make a piece of wood more desirable for some uses, particularly when they produce a visually stunning figure such as bird's-eye. If their strength is not compromised, defective boards can be used for concealed parts to greatly reduce a project's cost.

In the end, it is the eventual use of the lumber that determines what is an acceptable blemish. By recognizing the lumber defects illustrated below and inspecting your wood carefully before buying you can increase your chances of getting the quality you want for the right price.

DEFECTS IN WOOD

TYPE	CHARACTERISTICS	REMEDIES
Knot 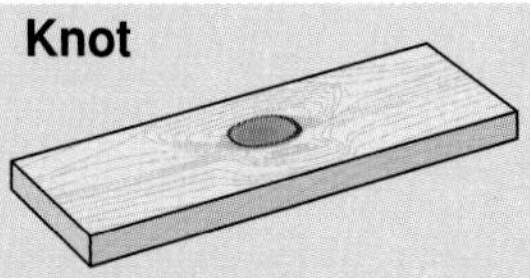	A tight knot appears as a whorl encircled by surrounding wood tissue; a dead knot is encircled by a dark ring. Formed as girth of tree increases, gradually enveloping the branches. Live branches integrate with surrounding wood; dead branch stumps cannot integrate and form dead knots.	Tight knots can be cut out or used, as appearance dictates; dead knots should be removed before working with stock.
Gum 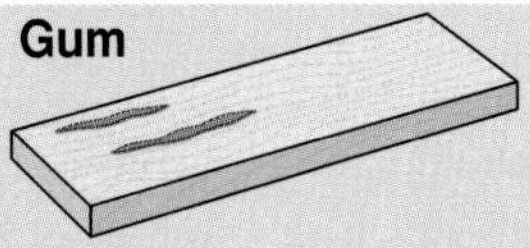	An accumulation of resin on the surface of the board or in pockets within the board. Usually develops when a tree has suffered an injury, exposure to fire, or insect attack.	Do not use stock if a quality finish is required, as gum will bleed through most finishes.
Checks 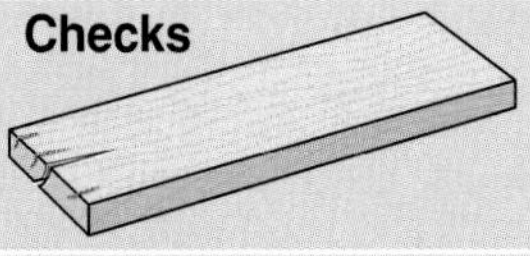	Lengthwise ruptures or separations in the wood, usually caused by rapid drying. Splits go right through board, from one face to the other. May compromise strength and appearance.	Can be cut off.
Bow 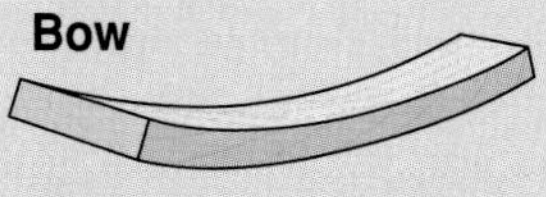	An end-to-end curve along the face, usually caused by improper storage. Introduces internal stresses in the wood that make it difficult to cut.	Flatten bowed boards on the jointer, or cut into shorter pieces, then use the jointer.
Cup 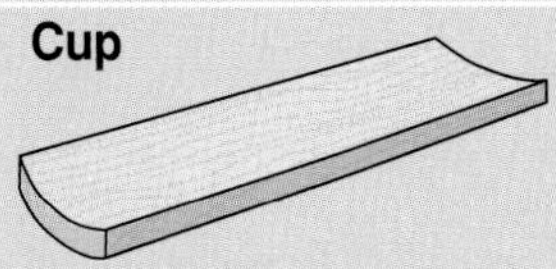	An edge-to-edge curve across the face. Common on tangentially cut stock, or boards cut close to the pith. Also occurs during drying if one face of a board has less contact with the air than the other.	Cup may correct itself if both faces are allowed to dry to the same moisture content. Cupped boards can be ripped into narrower ones on the band saw or flattened on the jointer.
Crook 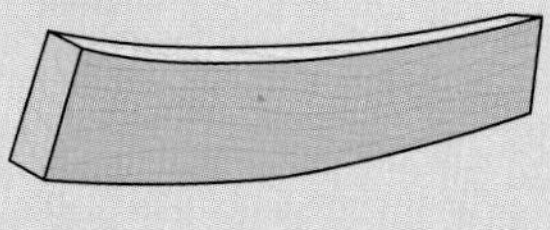	End-to-end curve along the edge, caused by incorrect seasoning or having the pith of a board close to the board edge. Weakens the wood, making it unsuitable for weight-bearing applications.	High spots can be flattened on jointer or cut off on table saw.
Twist 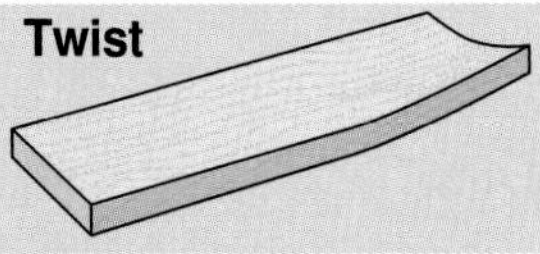	Uneven or irregular warping where one corner is not aligned with the others. Results from uneven drying or a cross grain pattern that is not parallel to the edge.	Board can be cut into shorter pieces.
Shake 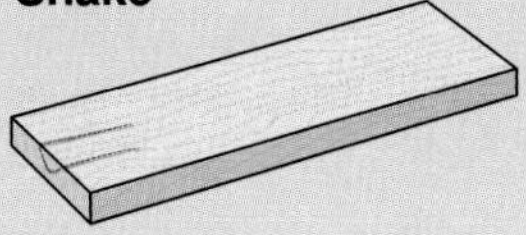	Lengthwise separation of the grain, usually between the growth rings. Results from improper drying of wood or felling damage.	Cut off shake, allowing for possibility that the defect may continue lengthwise under the surface.

PREPARING STOCK

SURFACING LUMBER

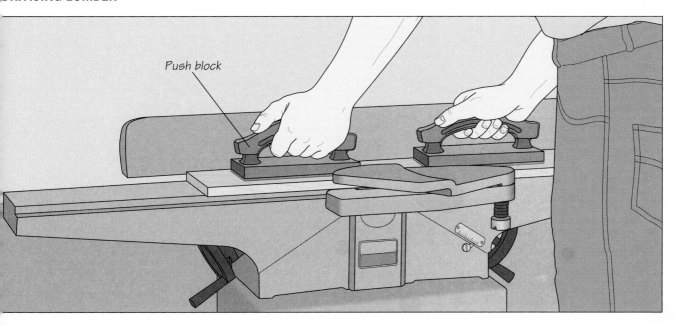

Push block

Jointing a board

If you are working with rough lumber, start by jointing one face. Lay the workpiece face down on the infeed table a few inches from the knives, butt its edge against the fence, and place two push blocks squarely on the top face, centered between the edges. (Use push blocks with angled handles to keep your hands from hitting the fence.) Feed the board slowly and steadily across the knives *(above)*, applying downward pressure to keep the board flat on the outfeed table, and lateral pressure to hold it flush against the fence. Next, joint an edge of the board. With the face you just jointed resting against the fence and the edge on the table, feed the board with a hand-over-hand technique. Next, plane the board *(step below)* to create two parallel faces.

Planing stock

Set the cutting depth to $\frac{1}{16}$ inch. Stand to one side of the workpiece and use both hands to feed the stock into the machine, keeping the edges of the board parallel to the planer table. Once the machine grips the board and begins to pull it across the cutterhead, support the trailing end to keep it flat on the table *(left)*. Then move to the outfeed side of the planer and support the workpiece with both hands until it clears the outfeed roller. To prevent stock from warping, avoid passing only one face of a board through the machine; instead, plane the same amount of wood from both sides.

CUTTING STOCK TO SIZE

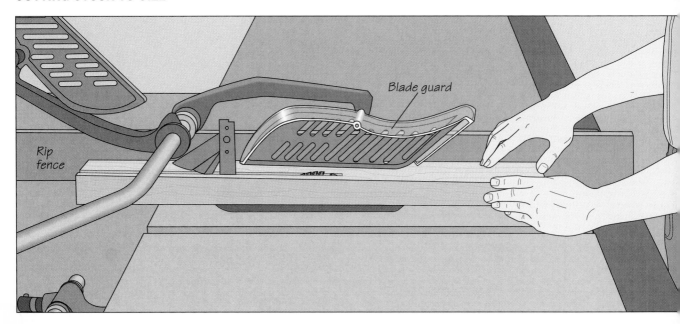

Ripping a workpiece

Rip stock to width on your table saw using the rip fence as a guide. Raise the blade to about ¼ inch above the workpiece. Position the rip fence for the width of cut, then feed the stock into the blade, pressing it against the fence with your left hand and pushing it with both thumbs *(above)*. Stand to the left of the workpiece and straddle the fence with your right hand, making certain that neither hand is in line with the blade. Once your fingers approach the blade, use a push stick to complete the pass. **(Caution: Blade guard partially retracted for clarity.)**

Crosscutting stock

Cut your stock to length on the table saw. With the workpiece flush against the miter gauge, align the cutting mark with the blade. Position the rip fence well away from the stock to prevent the cut-off piece from jamming between the blade and fence, and kicking back toward you. Hook your thumbs over the miter gauge, hold the board against the gauge and flat on the table, then feed the board across the table *(right)*. **(Caution: Blade guard partially retracted for clarity.)**

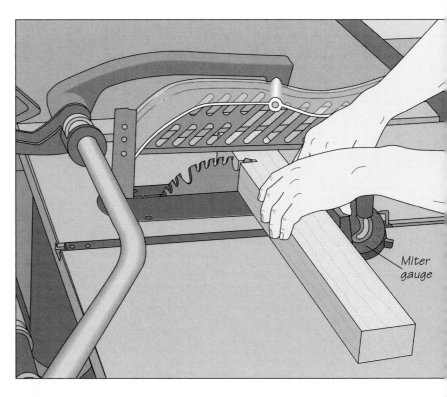

DESIGNING TABLES AND DESKS

A crucial part of building a piece of furniture is deciding on its final dimensions. A desk that is too high or low will be uncomfortable; a tabletop that crowds its diners will make mealtime an aggravating experience. Once you have chosen a particular style from the gallery of tables and desks starting on page 22, it is time to size its parts. Standard dimensions for a wide range of traditional and modern table and desk styles are provided below. Dining tables should provide 24 inches in width for each diner. Allow at least 12 inches from the table edge to the center for each place setting; an additional 4 to 6 inches will provide space for serving dishes. To allow adequate leg room, leave about 7 ½ inches between the chair seat and the underside of the top, and at least 2 feet between the floor and the bottom of the table or desk rail. Remember, however, that these figures are guidelines; furniture should fit those using it.

A table or a desk also should fit into its environment. For desks and dining tables, remember to allow for the height of the accompanying chairs. Bedside tables should not rise more than 6 inches above the bed.

STANDARD TABLE AND DESK DIMENSIONS

TABLES	HEIGHT	LENGTH	WIDTH	DIAMETER
Bedside (night table)	24" - 30"	18"	18"	—
Butler's table	24" - 36"	36" - 48"	20"	—
Butterfly table	Depends on use	Depends on use	Depends on use	—
Candle stand	25" - 31"	—	—	12" - 17"
Card table	25" - 29"	28" - 36"	28" - 36"	—
Coffee table	12" - 22"	Depends on use	20"	—
Conference table	30"	Depends on use	Depends on use	—
Console table	30"	36" - 72"	16" - 20"	—
Dressing table	29" - 30"	40" - 48"	18" - 22"	—
Drop-leaf table	Depends on use	Depends on use	Depends on use	—
Extension dining table	29" - 31"	Open: 96"; closed: 60"	36" - 42"	—
Gateleg table	29" - 30"	Depends on use	Depends on use	Depends on use
Library table	30"	60" - 84"	24" - 36"	—
Occasional table	27" - 29"	24" - 28"	24" - 28"	24" - 28"
Round dining table	29" - 31"	—	—	At least 40"
Tilt-top table	26" - 28"	—	—	24" - 26"
Trestle table	29" - 31"	48" - 120"	At least 30"	—
DESKS				
Computer desk	20" - 26"	48" - 50"	24" - 30"	—
Executive desk	29" - 30"	72" - 84"	36" - 42"	—
Office desk	29"	60"	30"	—
Pedestal desk	30"	30" - 42"	18" - 22"	—
Secretarial desk	30"	60" - 66"	30" - 32"	—
Secretary	Total height: 74" - 86"; Writing surface: 29" - 30"	30" - 44" —	18" - 22" —	— —
Typewriter stand	30"	30"	18"	—

TABLE AND DESK STYLES

Hundreds of table and desk styles have evolved throughout the ages, each with its own specific purpose. The butler's table, for example, also serves as a serving tray. The secretary *(page 26)* combines a bookcase, a desk, and a chest of drawers, supplying ample storage space for books, papers, and other items, and a writing surface that can be folded up out of the way when not in use. The following pages illustrate more than two dozen types of tables and desks to inspire your designs.

The knockdown trestle table is a design that traces its roots back to the Middle Ages. The example shown above was built from cherry by Thos. Moser Cabinetmakers in Auburn, Maine.

Card table
A square table, sometimes with dished corners for holding coins. One side is normally left undecorated and placed against a wall when the table is not in use. The top folds in half and the side rails fold inward to move the legs closer together

Butterfly table
An American drop-leaf table, utilizing a pivoting support to hold up wide leaves on either side of a narrow, central tabletop

Coffee table
A low occasional table designed to be used with sofa and chairs

Butler's table
A portable table, the sides and ends of which fold up to form a gallery, or fence, and handles

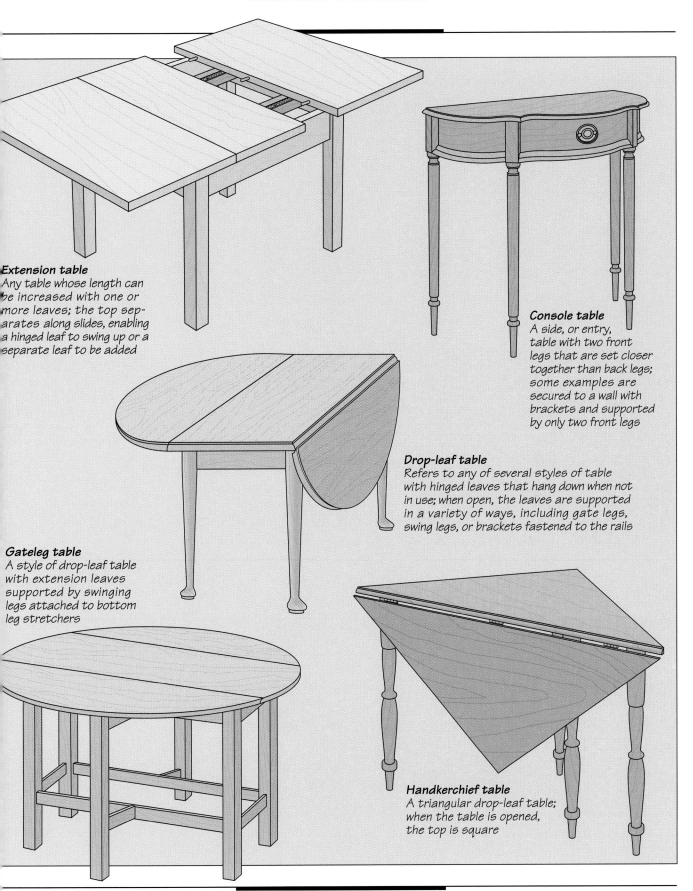

Extension table
Any table whose length can be increased with one or more leaves; the top separates along slides, enabling a hinged leaf to swing up or a separate leaf to be added

Console table
A side, or entry, table with two front legs that are set closer together than back legs; some examples are secured to a wall with brackets and supported by only two front legs

Drop-leaf table
Refers to any of several styles of table with hinged leaves that hang down when not in use; when open, the leaves are supported in a variety of ways, including gate legs, swing legs, or brackets fastened to the rails

Gateleg table
A style of drop-leaf table with extension leaves supported by swinging legs attached to bottom leg stretchers

Handkerchief table
A triangular drop-leaf table; when the table is opened, the top is square

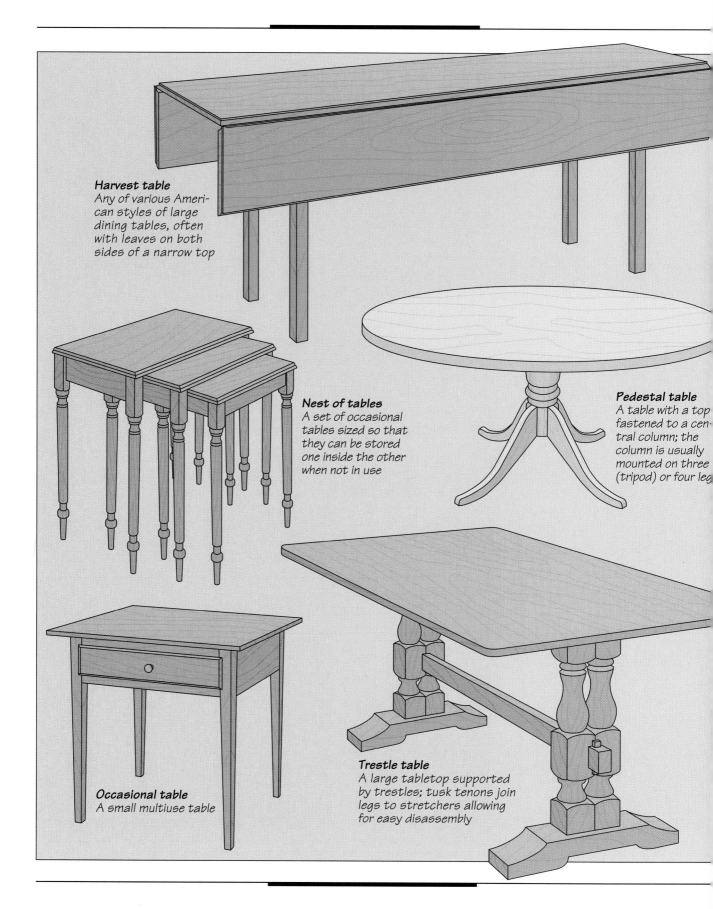

Harvest table
Any of various American styles of large dining tables, often with leaves on both sides of a narrow top

Nest of tables
A set of occasional tables sized so that they can be stored one inside the other when not in use

Pedestal table
A table with a top fastened to a central column; the column is usually mounted on three (tripod) or four legs

Occasional table
A small multiuse table

Trestle table
A large tabletop supported by trestles; tusk tenons join legs to stretchers allowing for easy disassembly

Stand
Any small table designed to display objects; a candle stand is one example

Tilt-top table
A variation of the tripod pedestal table featuring a top that pivots vertically to conserve space

Pembroke table
A type of drop-leaf table with leaves supported by brackets hinged to the table rails; commonly features one or two drawers

Night table
A small occasional table used to support lamps and other bedside accessories; often with one or more drawers and a shelf or small storage compartment

Tavern table
Low rectangular or circular table with stretchers and turned legs; occasionally, the table has carved supports at the ends connected by a stretcher

Seattle craftsman Hank Holtzer built the "Morrison table" shown above from walnut. The extension table features a 5-foot-diameter top that opens to 8 feet. It will seat from 6 to 10 people.

Fall-front desk
A desk with a working surface that "falls" down into the open position, held up by supports that slide out of recesses in the desk front

Secretary
A style of slant-top desk featuring a fall-front writing surface with a chest of drawers below and a bookcase with wood or glass doors above

Pedestal desk (kneehole type)
Features a top supported on both sides by drawer carcases called pedestals; the kneehole is closed at the back and may contain a shallow cupboard

Writing table
Any flat-topped desk with a writing surface and drawers below the top

Lap desk
A small lift-top desk held on the lap while in use

Writing desk
Also known by the British term Davenport, this small desk has an angled, lifting top with storage space under it; drawers or cupboards are located on the sides of the carcase, rather than in the front

Pedestal desk (partner's type)
Similar to the kneehole pedestal desk, but the top is larger and the gap between the pedestals is left open on both sides—originally to allow two people to use the desk at the same time

Roll-top desk
A desk with a sliding cover, or tambour, that can be drawn down to cover the writing surface; the top may be supported by pedestals or legs

Standing desk
Also known as a clerk's desk, this tall, slanting lift-top desk typically has one or two small drawers and may have a shelf below the writing surface

Suggestive of an open fall-front desk, the piece shown at left incorporates other design elements, including a graceful curve along the front edge of the top. The desk was built from cherry and maple by Judith Ames of Seattle.

DESK CASEWORK

Gluing up a large carcase requires many clamps. In the setup shown above, bar clamps are aligned with the panels of the carcase and with the dust frames being joined to the carcase sides. Applying uniform pressure on all of the joints will help make the carcase square and solid.

Casework is the fundamental building block of most desks. It can be as simple as a four-sided box or as elaborate as a frame-and-panel cabinet. Such elements as dividers, shelves, drawers, face frames, and dust panels provide refinements that transform this casework into a piece of furniture.

This chapter will show you how to apply casework techniques to the construction of a two-pedestal desk like the one shown opposite. Carcases are easier to build than frame-and-panel cabinets. As shown on page 30, all carcases consist of four panels joined to form a box. Make sure that the wood grain of all the panels runs in the same direction. This will allow the panels to swell and shrink at the same rate as relative humidity levels change. If you assemble a carcase with the grain of adjacent panels at right angles to each other you risk splitting one of the panels.

The second type of casework—frame-and-panel—solves the problem of wood movement by allowing space for swelling and shrinkage. As illustrated on page 31, individual frame-and-panel assemblies are joined to form a case. The opening in each frame is filled by a panel that rests in grooves cut in the inside edges of the frame. Although the frame pieces are glued together at the corners, the panel is set into the frames without adhesive to allow it to swell and shrink. The panel is often beveled around the edges—a decorative touch that also allows it to fit more easily into its groove.

The method you choose for assembling a carcase or frame-and-panel case will influence the character and individuality of your desk. Various joinery options are shown on page 32. The rabbet joint works well with either solid wood or plywood panels. Through dovetails are more time-consuming to make but they are more attractive and considered a sign of fine craftsmanship. Frame-and-panel assemblies can be put together with mortise-and-tenons or the more decorative cope-and-stick joint.

The double-pedestal desk shown at left features two identical carcases joined together by rails, which are concealed by the top. The pedestals sit on molded bases and are divided by dust frames to accommodate drawers.

TWO TYPES OF DESK CASEWORK

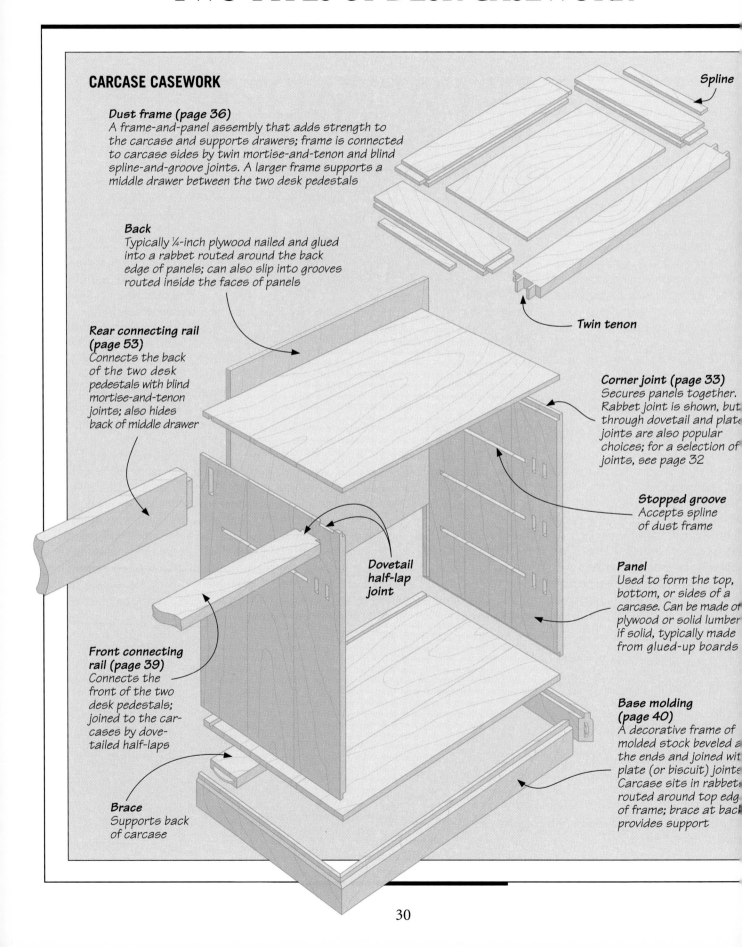

CARCASE CASEWORK

Dust frame (page 36)
A frame-and-panel assembly that adds strength to the carcase and supports drawers; frame is connected to carcase sides by twin mortise-and-tenon and blind spline-and-groove joints. A larger frame supports a middle drawer between the two desk pedestals

Back
Typically ¼-inch plywood nailed and glued into a rabbet routed around the back edge of panels; can also slip into grooves routed inside the faces of panels

Rear connecting rail (page 53)
Connects the back of the two desk pedestals with blind mortise-and-tenon joints; also hides back of middle drawer

Front connecting rail (page 39)
Connects the front of the two desk pedestals; joined to the carcases by dovetailed half-laps

Brace
Supports back of carcase

Dovetail half-lap joint

Spline

Twin tenon

Corner joint (page 33)
Secures panels together. Rabbet joint is shown, but through dovetail and plate joints are also popular choices; for a selection of joints, see page 32

Stopped groove
Accepts spline of dust frame

Panel
Used to form the top, bottom, or sides of a carcase. Can be made of plywood or solid lumber if solid, typically made from glued-up boards

Base molding (page 40)
A decorative frame of molded stock beveled a the ends and joined wit plate (or biscuit) jointe Carcase sits in rabbet routed around top edg of frame; brace at back provides support

FRAME-AND-PANEL CASEWORK

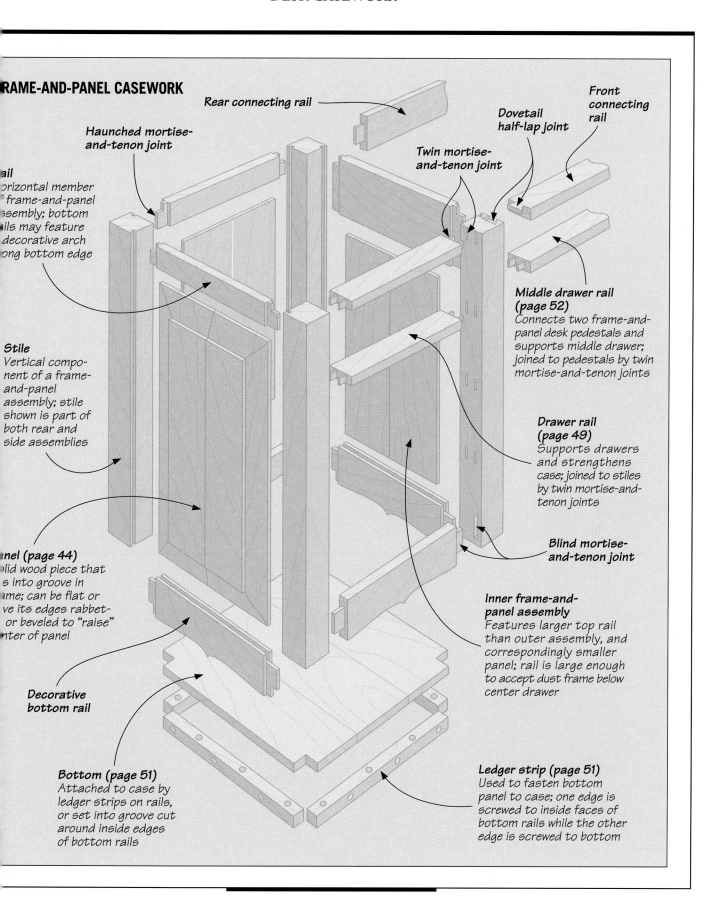

Rear connecting rail

Haunched mortise-and-tenon joint

Twin mortise-and-tenon joint

Dovetail half-lap joint

Front connecting rail

ail
orizontal member
frame-and-panel
ssembly; bottom
ils may feature
decorative arch
ong bottom edge

Stile
Vertical compo-
nent of a frame-
and-panel
assembly; stile
shown is part of
both rear and
side assemblies

nel (page 44)
lid wood piece that
s into groove in
ame; can be flat or
ve its edges rabbet-
or beveled to "raise"
nter of panel

**Decorative
bottom rail**

**Middle drawer rail
(page 52)**
Connects two frame-and-
panel desk pedestals and
supports middle drawer;
joined to pedestals by twin
mortise-and-tenon joints

**Drawer rail
(page 49)**
Supports drawers
and strengthens
case; joined to stiles
by twin mortise-and-
tenon joints

**Blind mortise-
and-tenon joint**

**Inner frame-and-
panel assembly**
Features larger top rail
than outer assembly, and
correspondingly smaller
panel; rail is large enough
to accept dust frame below
center drawer

Bottom (page 51)
Attached to case by
ledger strips on rails,
or set into groove cut
around inside edges
of bottom rails

Ledger strip (page 51)
Used to fasten bottom
panel to case; one edge is
screwed to inside faces of
bottom rails while the other
edge is screwed to bottom

CASEWORK JOINTS

Rabbet joint (page 33)
Used to join carcase panels together; end of one panel fits into rabbet cut in the mating panel. Rabbet is typically routed in carcase sides to conceal end grain of top and bottom panels

Twin mortise-and-tenon (page 34)
Used to join dust panels to carcase sides and drawer rails to frame-and-panel stiles

Blind mortise-and-tenon (page 36)
Used to assemble dust frames and connect desk pedestals together; connects rails and stiles in frame-and-panel assemblies

Stopped groove-and-spline (page 37)
Used to join stretchers and dust panels to carcase sides. Stopped grooves are routed in both the edge of the stretcher or the dust frame rail and the inside face of the carcase side; a floating spline allows for wood movement

Stopped tongue-and-dado joint
An alternative to the stopped groove-and-spline for attaching stretchers to carcase sides; a stopped tongue cut in edge of stretcher fits into stopped groove cut in carcase

Dovetailed half-lap (page 39)
Made on connecting rails to join desk pedestals

Beveled plate joint (page 40)
Used to assemble pieces of base molding together; biscuits of compressed wood fit into slots cut in beveled ends of mating surfaces

Haunched mortise-and-tenon (page 41)
Used to join rails and stiles in frame-and-panel assemblies; tenon haunch in rail fills panel grooves routed in stiles

Plate (biscuit) joint
Used to join carcase panels together without having to shape the pieces; biscuits of compressed wood fit into slots cut in the mating boards. Slots are typically cut into ends of top and bottom panels

Cope-and-stick joint
A decorative alternative to blind and haunched mortise-and-tenons for frame-and-panel construction. A set of router bits cuts matching profiles in rails and stiles; groove for floating panel is cut simultaneously

Through dovetails (page 125)
Tapered pins on top and bottom panels interlock with angled tails cut into the side panels; used where the joinery is an important element of design

BUILDING A CARCASE

Four panels joined to form a box: The carcase is the simplest and most basic building block of furniture construction. A carcase provides the rigid framework for items as diverse as a bookcase and a drawer. Build two boxes and join them together and you have the heart of an attractive two-pedestal desk. The section that follows shows how to do this.

Carcase panels can be constructed from plywood, but for fine furniture, the panels are most frequently made from narrow boards edge-glued into wider panels *(page 93)*. The panels are then planed, jointed on one edge, cut to size, and sanded. To allow the panels to contract and expand with changes in humidity, the grain of all panels in a carcase is aligned in the same direction.

The twin mortise-and-tenon joint offers more gluing surface and structural stability than a simple mortise-and-tenon, and is often used to join stretchers to carcase sides. Here a twin tenon is being test-fitted into its mating mortises in the side of a desk.

Carcases can be assembled with several types of joints *(page 32)*. The rabbet joint is a popular choice: The joint offers a large gluing surface and is simple to make. As illustrated below, the rabbets are best cut into the side panels so that the end grain of the top and bottom panels will be covered. The end grain of the sides is often concealed by the top.

When planning a carcase, it is wise to take into consideration the type of shelving or drawers *(page 116)* that will be built into it. For example, the desk shown on page 28 features dust frames *(page 34)* that both support the drawers and provide strength to the carcase. The joinery needs of these frames must be taken into account before the carcase is glued up.

PREPARING THE SIDES: RABBET JOINTS

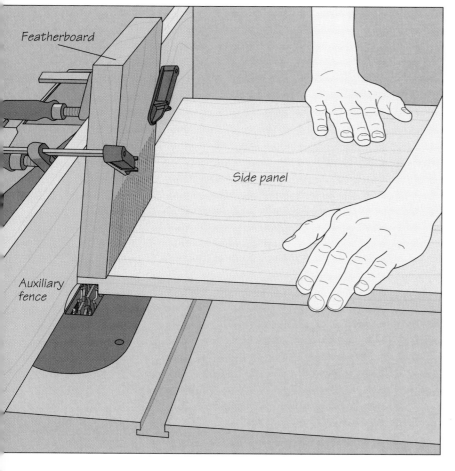

Featherboard

Side panel

Auxiliary fence

1 Cutting rabbets in the carcase sides
The rabbet width should equal the thickness of the carcase top; mark a cutting line for the rabbets on the leading edge of one side panel. Install a dado head slightly wider than the rabbet on your table saw. Attach an auxiliary wood fence to the rip fence and raise the dado head to cut a notch in the wood fence. Set the cutting height at one-half the stock thickness and adjust the fence for the width of cut. Clamp a featherboard to the fence directly above the blade to hold the panel securely against the table, then make the cut *(left)*. Cut a rabbet at the opposite end of the panel and both ends of the other side panel.

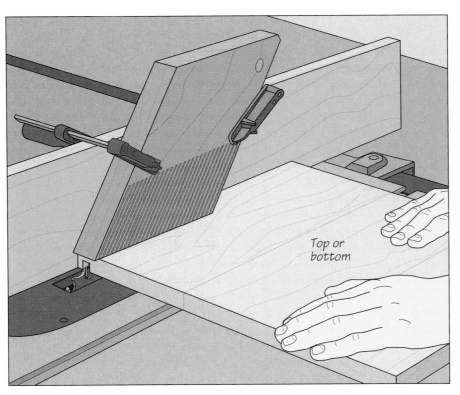

2 **Cutting grooves for the back panel**
Once you have rabbeted the carcase sides, you need to prepare the four panels to accommodate the back, which can be set into a rabbet or a groove. For the rabbet, repeat step 1, but make the cut along the back edge of each panel and adjust the cutting depth to the thickness of the back—typically ¼ inch. For the groove, adjust the dado head to a width of ¼ inch, then position the fence so the groove will be ¼ inch from the back edge of the panel (*left*). Cut the back from ¼-inch plywood to fit the opening in the carcase, adding the depth of the grooves to its dimensions.

Top or bottom

MAKING DUST FRAMES

1 **Cutting twin tenons in the front rails**
The dust frames that will support the drawers are joined to the desk pedestals with twin mortise-and-tenon joints (*page 36*). Start by cutting the tenons in each front rail on your table saw; they will fit into matching mortises in the carcase side panels (*step 3*). Equip your table saw with a dado head ¼ inch wide, then install a tenoning jig in the miter slot. Mark a twin tenon at each end of the rail, and set the cutting height at ½ inch. Clamp the rail to the jig end-up and shift the jig sideways to align one of the tenon marks with the dado head. To make the cut, push the jig forward, feeding the stock into the blades (*right*). Turn the rail around to cut the other tenon shoulder. Repeat the cuts at the other end of the rail and at both ends of the remaining rails.

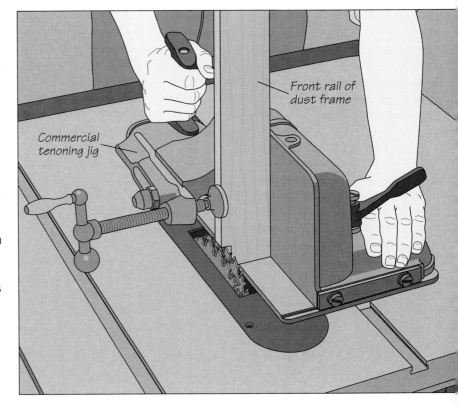

Commercial tenoning jig

Front rail of dust frame

2 Clearing the waste between tenons
Shift the tenoning jig to line up the dado head with the waste between the twin tenons *(right)*. Make several passes until you have cleared away the excess wood.

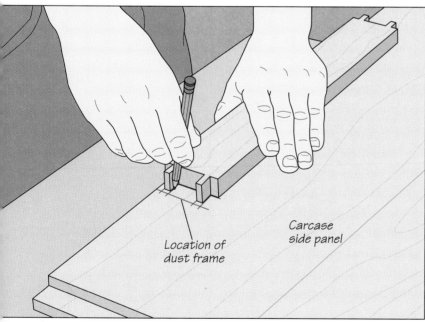

Location of dust frame

Carcase side panel

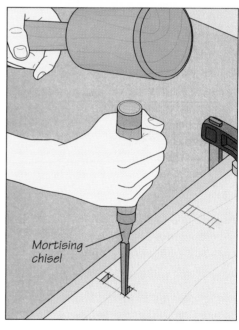

Mortising chisel

3 Chiseling the double mortises in the carcase sides
Mark lines on the inside face of the side panel for the location of each dust panel. Place the rail face down on the panel, aligning the edges of both and positioning the end of the rail flush with the top line. Outline the twin tenons on the panel *(above, left)*. Repeat for the other rails. To chop out the mortises, clamp the panel to a work surface. Then, starting at an end of one outline, hold a mortising chisel square to the face of the panel and strike the handle with a wooden mallet. Use a chisel the same width as the mortises and be sure that the beveled side is facing the waste. Continue making cuts at intervals of about ⅛ inch until you reach the other end of the outline. Use the chisel to lever out the waste to the required depth. Chop out the adjacent mortise *(above, right)* and the other double mortises the same way. Test-fit the joint and widen or deepen the mortise with the chisel, as required.

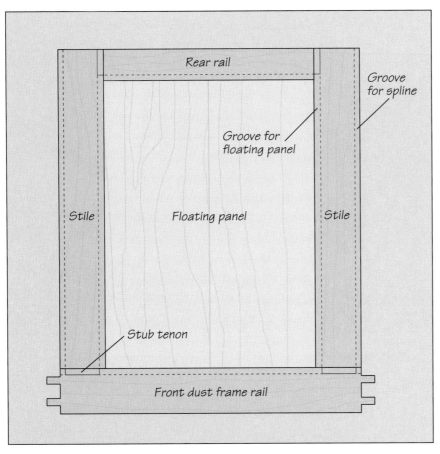

Rear rail

Groove
for spline

Groove for
floating panel

Stile

Floating panel

Stile

Stub tenon

Front dust frame rail

Making the dust frames

4 Prepare a rear rail, a floating ¼" plywood panel, and two stiles for each dust frame as you would for a non-raised frame-and-panel assembly *(page 48)*, sizing the frame to fit the interior of the carcase. Instead of cutting rabbets, rout a ¼-inch-deep groove around the inside edge of the frame to accommodate the panel; the grooves will also serve as mortises for the stub tenons that join the rails and stiles together. Also rout a groove along the outside edge of each stile to accept the spline that will fit into a matching groove in a carcase side panel *(page 37)*.

Gluing up the dust frames

5 Sand any surfaces of the frame that will be difficult to reach after glue up. Spread adhesive on the tenons and their mating grooves. Do not apply glue in the panel groove; the panel must be free to move. Glue one of the stiles to one of the rails, insert the panel, then assemble the other pieces. Clamp the dust frame across the joints with bar clamps, checking for square and using wood pads to protect the stock *(below)*.

Wood
pad

GLUING UP THE CARCASE

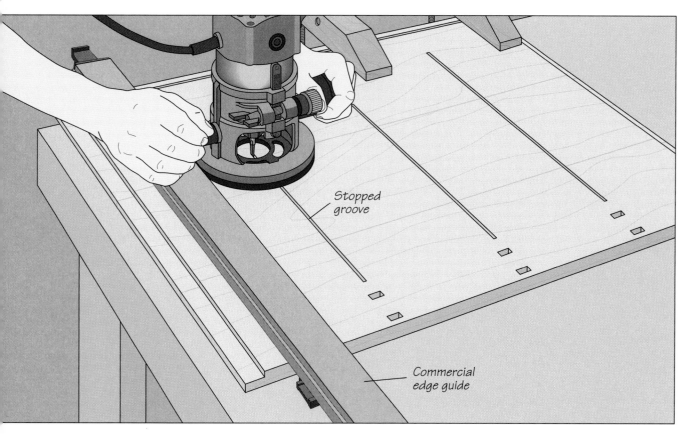

Stopped groove

Commercial edge guide

SHOP TIP

Screwing drawer-support frames to a carcase
If you are installing support frames, wood screws offer a quick and easy way to fix them to the sides of a carcase. Use two screws to secure each frame stile in place. Bore an elongated clearance hole (page 96) for each screw through the stile and into the carcase side, making sure the two holes for the same stile are perfectly aligned.

1 Grooving the carcase sides
Each dust frame is secured to the carcase sides with stopped groove-and-spline joints that will enable the frame to move with changes in humidity. Each joint consists of a hardwood spline that will sit in matching stopped grooves routed in the carcase side and the stile of the dust frame. To cut the grooves in the carcase, install a ¼-inch straight bit in your router and secure one of the side panels inside-face up to a work surface. Clamp an edge guide to the panel so the bit will be centered on one of the double mortises you cut for the drawer rails. For each dust frame, rout a stopped groove starting about 1 inch from the mortises (above) and stopping about 3 inches from the opposite edge. Repeat for the other carcase side.

Spline

2 Installing the dust frames

Cut two hardwood or plywood splines for each frame. The splines should be a little shorter than the grooves you cut in step 1 to allow for wood movement; for maximum strength, the grain should run across the spline's width. Place one side of the carcase inside-face up on a work surface, apply glue to the twin mortises and tenons, and set the frames in place, making sure that they fit snugly over the splines *(left)*.

3 Assembling the carcase

With all the dust frames in place and the remaining splines set in their grooves, assemble the rest of the carcase. First apply glue along the rabbets in one side panel and slide the back and bottom in position *(right)*. Next, set the top in place. Spread some glue on the remaining twin mortise-and-tenons and carefully lower the other side panel on top of the assembly, guiding the splines into their grooves and the twin tenons into their mortises. Install bar clamps across the front of the carcase, aligned with each dust frame, and across both the top and bottom of the assembly. Use wood pads to protect the stock. Reinforce the rabbet joints and the back with countersunk nails or screws which can later be concealed with plugs.

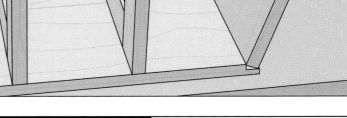

Back

Bottom

INSTALLING A CONNECTING RAIL

1 Cutting dovetailed half-laps in the front connecting rail

In a two-pedestal desk, the carcases are joined by connecting rails and a dust frame that supports a central drawer. The front connecting rail is joined to the carcases with dovetailed half-lap joints. To prepare each rail, cut it to size and saw a dovetailed half-lap in each end with a dovetail saw *(right)*.

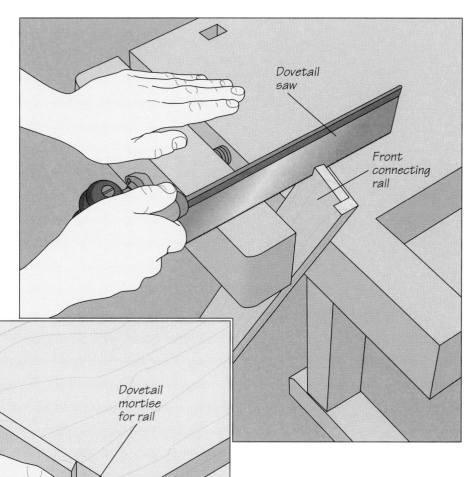

Dovetail saw

Front connecting rail

Spline groove for central dust frame

Dovetail mortise for rail

Twin mortises for central dust frame

2 Cutting the mating dovetails in the carcases

Use one of the dovetailed half-laps you cut in step 1 to outline the mating dovetail mortise in each carcase. Then use a saw and chisel to cut the mortise *(left)*. Next, make a dust frame *(page 36)* to fit between the carcases and support the central drawer. Rout grooves and mortises on the outside of both carcases to accommodate the joinery. Also cut a rail to span the carcases at the back and hide the back of the drawer *(page 53)*. Join this rail to the carcases with blind mortise-and-tenon joints. Assemble and clamp the desk together *(page 53)*.

BASE MOLDING

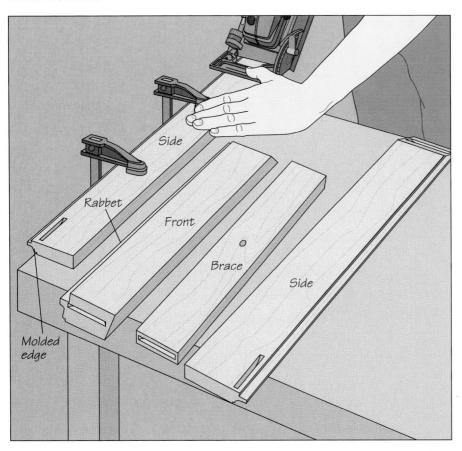

1 Making the base molding

The base molding for the carcase is made from three pieces of molded stock and a brace. To prepare the molding, rout a decorative detail along one edge of each board, using your table saw fitted with a molding cutter head or a table-mounted router with a molding bit. Then cut a rabbet in each piece along the opposite side of the same edge; this will form a lip to support the carcase. Saw the boards to length, beveling both ends of the front piece and only the front end of the sides. Also saw a bracing piece that will fit, face-up, between the sides at the back of the molding; bore a hole for a screw through the brace. The screw will attach the brace to the carcase. The molding in the illustration is assembled with plate joints. The boards will mate end-to-end, except at the back of the molding, where the brace is joined to the inside faces of the sides. A plate joiner with an adjustable fence makes it easier to align the tool when cutting the slots in the beveled ends *(left)*.

2 Gluing up the base molding

Working quickly, apply glue to all the slots, insert one biscuit for each joint, and assemble the base molding. Secure the brace to the sides with a bar clamp, using wood pads to protect the stock; install a web clamp with corner brackets around the molding at the miter joints. Tighten the web clamp, using the wrench provided *(right)*, then tighten the bar clamp. Once the glue is dry, install the base by applying glue only along the rabbet in the front piece and set the carcase in place. (This will cause any wood movement in the side pieces to take place towards the back of the molding, preventing the miters at the front from separating.) Attach the brace to the carcase by driving a screw through the hole you drilled in step 1.

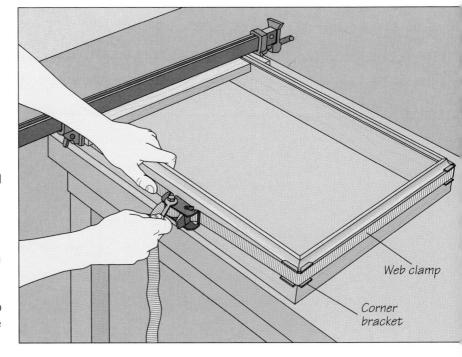

Web clamp

Corner bracket

BUILDING A FRAME-AND-PANEL DESK

Frame-and-panel construction offers one solution to the perennial problem of wood movement. The principle is simple: A panel "floats" in a groove cut on the inside edge of a frame. The panel can be flat, as in a dust frame (page 48), or "raised," with bevels cut along its edge. The beveling allows the panel to fit into a groove in the frame and presents a decorative face to the public. A panel can be raised on the router table (page 44) or the table saw (page 45).

To construct a frame-and-panel desk like the one shown on page 31, you need to join four individual frame-and-panel assemblies: a rear assembly (page 47), a front assembly with drawer slides (page 49), four side rails, and two side panels. (The stiles in the front and rear assemblies double as stiles for the side frames.)

Traditionally, panels for frame-and-panel construction were "raised," or beveled, with specialized hand planes—a time-consuming task. Modern power tools, like a table saw with a tilting arbor, have made this operation much simpler.

HAUNCHED MORTISE-AND-TENON JOINTS

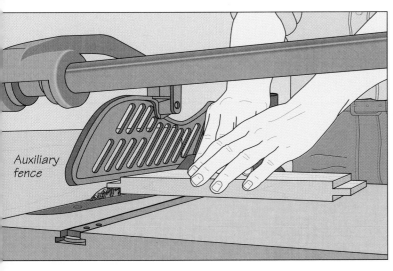

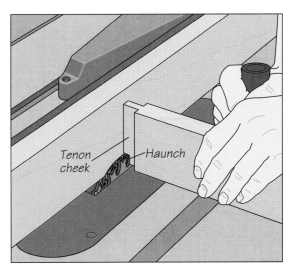

1 Cutting tenons in the rails

To join the rails and stiles of individual frame-and-panel assemblies with haunched mortise-and-tenons, install a dado head slightly wider than the length of the tenons on your table saw. Attach an auxiliary fence and raise the dado head to notch it. Set the width of cut equal to the tenon length. To cut the tenon cheeks, butt the stock against the fence and the miter gauge, then feed it face down. Turn the rail over and repeat the cut on the other side. Next, cut tenon cheeks at the other end of each rail (above, left). Position the fence to leave a haunch equal in width to the depth of the groove for the panel; set the height of the dado head to cut about ½ inch into the tenon. With the stock on edge, use the fence and miter gauge to guide it into the blade (above, right). Repeat to cut the haunch on the other side of the tenon. For the rails of the front assembly, which has no panel, cut blind tenons (page 42), making the shoulders equal to the width of the notch you cut into the haunched tenons.

BUILD IT YOURSELF

A TENONING JIG FOR THE TABLE SAW

You can use the jig shown at right to cut blind tenons on the table saw. Adapt the dimensions suggested in the illustration to customize the jig for your saw, if necessary.

Cut the jig fence and back from ¾-inch plywood and saw a 45° bevel at one end of each board; the pieces should be wider than the height of your saw's rip fence. Fasten two pieces together face to face to fashion the back, then use countersunk screws to attach the fence and back in an L shape. Make sure the fasteners will not be in the blade's path when you use the jig. Next, cut the brace from solid stock, bevel its ends, and attach it flush with the top edges of the fence and back, forming a triangle. Make the clamp by face gluing two pieces of ¾-inch plywood and cutting the assembly into the shape shown. Use a hanger bolt, washer, and wing nut to attach the clamp to the jig back, leaving a gap between the edge of the clamp and the fence equal to the thickness of the stock you will use. Offset the bolt so the clamp can pivot eccentrically. (You can drill additional holes in the jig back so you can shift the clamp to accommodate different stock thicknesses.) Next, cut the runner from solid wood. When attached to the jig fence, the runner will straddle the saw fence, eliminating any wobble. For some models, you will have to mill a groove down the length of the runner, as shown, to fit the rip fence. Finally, cut a piece of clear plastic as a blade guard and screw it to the jig back flush with its front face.

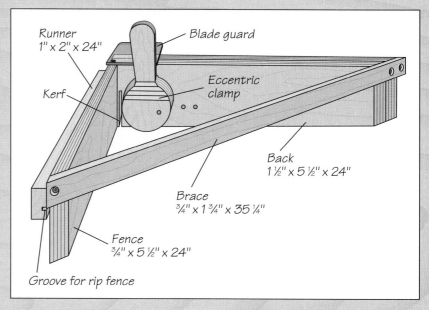

Runner
1" x 2" x 24"

Blade guard

Kerf

Eccentric clamp

Back
1 ½" x 5 ½" x 24"

Brace
¾" x 1 ¾" x 35 ¼"

Fence
¾" x 5 ½" x 24"

Groove for rip fence

To use the jig, set it on the saw table in front of the blade with the runner and fence straddling the rip fence. Clamp the workpiece in the jig and position the rip fence to align the cutting mark on the workpiece with the blade. Feed the jig into the cutting edge. (Your first use of the jig will produce a kerf in the back.) Flip the workpiece around and repeat to cut the other cheek (*below*). Remove the jig to cut the shoulders.

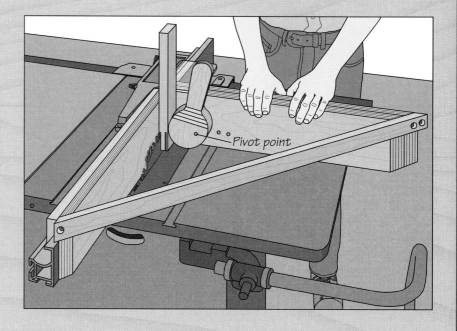

Pivot point

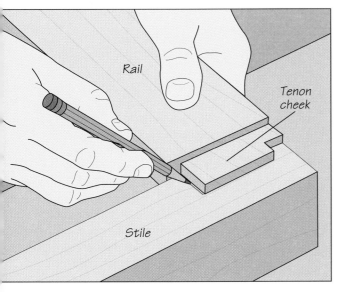

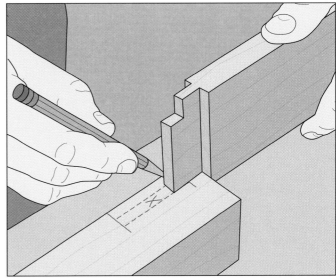

2 Outlining the mortises in the stiles

Mark the approximate locations of the mortises on each stile. (See page 52 for an overhead view.) Then use one of the rails you cut in step 1 to outline the length and width of the mortises. Start by holding the cheek of the tenon flush against the face of one of the stiles; make sure that the edge of the rail is aligned with the end of the stile. Outline the length of the tenon *(above, left)*. To mark the mortise width, hold the edge of a tenon flush against the marked face of the stile and outline the cheeks of the tenon *(above, right)*. Extend the lines along the face (shown in the illustration as dotted lines). Once all the mortises are outlined, chisel them out slightly deeper than the tenon length, using a mortise chisel *(page 35)*.

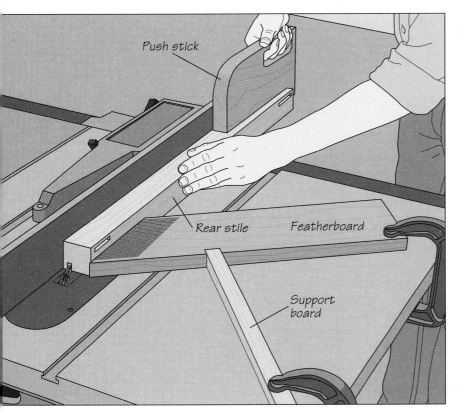

3 Cutting grooves for the panels

On the rails and stiles, mark locations for the grooves that will hold the panel. You will need to make a groove in two sides of each rear stile, aligning the cuts with the mortises you cut in step 2. Then set up your table saw with a dado head the same width as the groove, typically ¼ inch. To cut the grooves in the rails, center the edge of a rail directly over the dado head and position the fence against the stock. Set the blade height to ½ inch. Use a featherboard, braced by a support board, to hold the workpiece against the fence during the cut. To cut the grooves in the stiles, do not move the fence, but adjust the position of the featherboard and support board. Feed the stock with a push stick *(left)*.

MAKING A RAISED PANEL ON THE ROUTER TABLE

Bit pilot

1 Setting the fence
Start by cutting the panel to size. Test-fit the rails and stiles of the frame, then measure the opening between them. Add ½ inch to each of the dimensions to allow the beveled edges of the panel to rest in the grooves routed in the frame; this will leave ¼ inch on each side to allow for wood movement. Then fit a router with a panel-raising bit and mount the tool in a table. To ensure that the cutting depth is uniform, position the fence in line with the edge of the bit pilot. With the tool switched off, place a scrap board along the fence. Adjust the fence until the bit pilot turns as the board touches it *(left)*. Set the router to make a shallow cut at first, typically ⅛ inch.

2 Making the cut
Lower the guard over the bit and turn on the router. To minimize tearout, cut the ends first, beveling the top and bottom of the panel. Feed the stock into the bit outside-face down, keeping it butted against the fence *(right)*. Repeat for the two sides. Test-fit the panel in the grooves you cut in the rails and stiles *(page 43)*. If the panel sits less than ¼ inch deep, increase the cutting depth by ¹⁄₁₆ inch and make another pass around the panel.

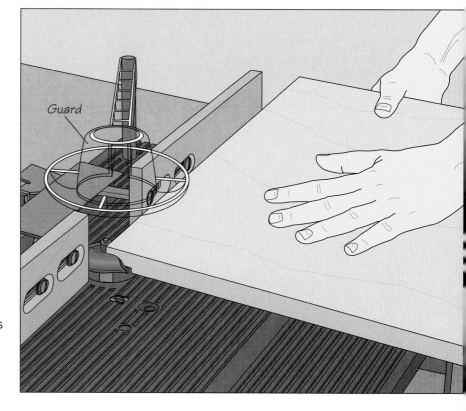

Guard

MAKING A RAISED PANEL ON THE TABLE SAW

1 Beveling the ends of the panel

Cut the panel to size, then set the blade angle to yield the proper bevel. The usual "reveal," or beveled area of a ¾-inch-thick panel is approximately 1¼ inches. For a ¼-inch-wide groove, begin by marking a ¼-inch square at the bottom corner of the panel. Then draw a line from the front face of the panel through the inside corner of the square to a point on the bottom edge ⅛ inch from the back face *(inset)*. Install a 5-inch-wide auxiliary wood fence, then adjust the angle of the blade and the position of the fence until the cutting edge aligns with the marked line. Next, raise the blade until one tooth protrudes beyond the front face of the panel. Clamp a guide block to the panel so it will ride along the top of the fence. Make a cut in one end of the panel *(right)*, and test-fit the cut in a groove. If the panel rests less than ¼ inch deep, move the fence a little closer to the blade and make another pass. Repeat the cut at the other end of the panel.

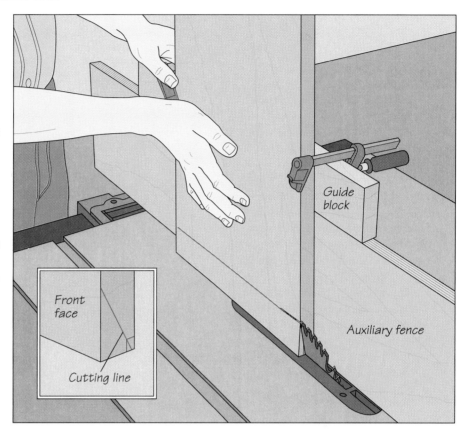

Guide block

Auxiliary fence

Front face

Cutting line

2 Beveling the sides

Beveling the sides after you have beveled the end grain helps minimize tearout. Set the panel on edge and feed it into the blade, keeping the back flush against the fence. Turn the panel over to cut the remaining edge *(left)*.

BUILD IT YOURSELF

A PANEL-RAISING JIG
FOR THE TABLE SAW

To raise a panel on the table saw without adjusting the angle of the blade, use the shop-built jig shown at right. Refer to the illustration for suggested dimensions.

Screw the lip along the bottom edge of the angled fence; make sure you position the screws where they will not interfere with the blade. Prop the angled fence against the auxiliary fence at the same angle as the cutting line marked on a panel *(page 45)*, using a sliding bevel to transfer the angle. Cut triangular supports to fit precisely between the two fences, then fix them in place with screws. Countersink the fasteners so the panel will slide smoothly along the angled fence.

To use the jig, position it on the saw table with the joint between the lip and the angled fence approximately ⅛ inch from the blade. Butt the table saw's rip fence against the jig's auxiliary fence, and screw the two together. Turn on the saw and crank up the blade slowly to cut a kerf through the lip. Next, seat the panel in the jig and adjust the height of the blade until a single tooth protrudes beyond the front of the panel. Make a test cut in a scrap board the same thickness as the panel and then check its fit in the groove; adjust the position of the fence or blade, if necessary. Then cut the panel, beveling the ends *(right, bottom)* before sawing the sides.

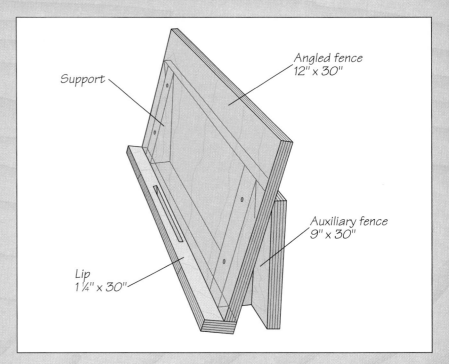

Support

Angled fence
12" x 30"

Auxiliary fence
9" x 30"

Lip
1¼" x 30"

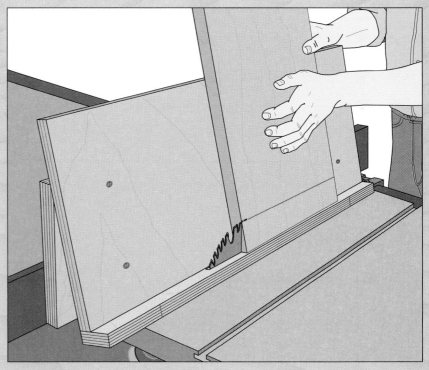

ASSEMBLING THE BACK FRAME-AND-PANEL

1 Fitting the panel in the frame

Once you have raised the panel, you are now ready to glue up the frame-and-panel assemblies that provide the backs of the two cases needed for a two-pedestal desk. Start by test-fitting the parts *(right)* and make any final adjustments. If any of the joints are too tight, use a chisel to pare away some wood. Once you are satisfied with the fit, disassemble the frame and sand any surfaces that will be difficult to reach once the assembly has been glued up. You should also decide which method you will use to install a top *page 96)*; some of these techniques require boring pocket holes in the rails or routing grooves in the rails and stiles.

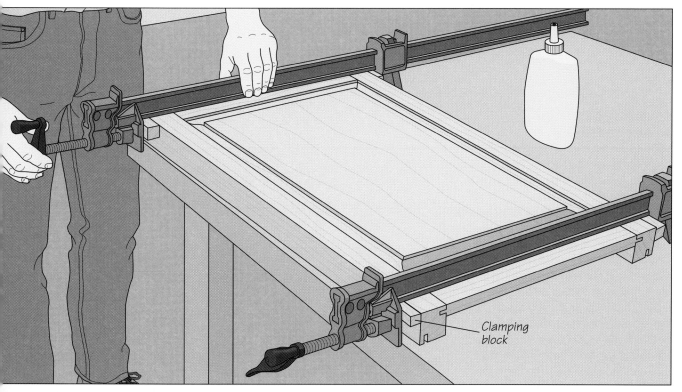

Clamping block

2 Gluing up

Apply glue to the tenon cheeks. Do not insert any adhesive in the grooves; the panel must be free to move. Clamp the frame and panel using bar clamps across the rails *(above),* protecting the stock with wood blocks the same width and thickness as the rails. Tighten each clamp in turn until a thin bead of glue squeezes out of the joints.

BUILDING A NON-RAISED FRAME AND PANEL

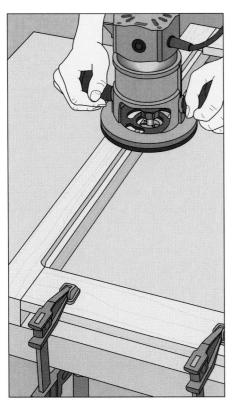

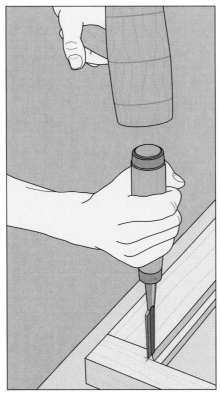

1 Routing a rabbet around the frame
Like dust frames *(page 34)*, the panels of frame-and-panel desks can be made flat instead of raised. To build this type of assembly, you can follow all the steps for a raised panel frame-and-panel *(page 41)*, except for beveling the edges of the panel. An alternative to placing the flat panel in a groove is to assemble the frame with blind mortise-and-tenons, and rout a rabbet around the frame to receive the panel. To cut the rabbet, glue up the rails and stiles and secure the assembly to a work surface. Install a ⅜-inch piloted rabbeting bit in your router. Set the depth of cut at least ¼ inch deeper than the thickness of your panel to leave room for decorative molding *(step 2)*. Rout the rabbet around the inside edges of the frame, keeping the bit pilot pressed against the stock throughout the cut *(far left)*, then square the corners with a chisel *(near left)*.

2 Installing the panel and decorative molding
Cut a panel from veneered plywood to fit the rabbets. (A solid-wood panel would split the frame, since the rabbets provide no room for wood movement.) Spread some glue in the rabbet and set the panel in place. For the decorative molding, shape the edge of a ¼-inch-thick board long enough to yield molding for the inside edges of your frame; make sure the board is wide enough to feed safely across the table saw or router table you use to shape the molding. Rip the molding from the board into ¼-inch-square pieces. Then cut four pieces to fit the inside the frame, mitering the ends. Glue the top and bottom strips of molding to the frame first, positioning them to hold the panel in place. To clamp the molding, use thin strips slightly longer than the gap between the molding pieces *(right)*.

Clamping strip

3 Installing molding along the panel sides

Once the glue securing the top and bottom molding strips has cured, glue the molding along the sides of the panel *(right)*. Again, use clamping strips to hold the molding in place.

Clamping strip

BUILDING A FRAME-AND-PANEL CASE

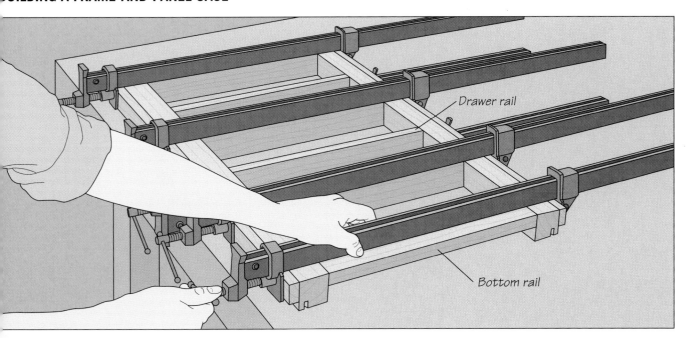

Drawer rail

Bottom rail

1 Gluing up the front assembly

To assemble a frame-and-panel pedestal for a desk, begin by gluing up the front frame. For the desk shown on page 31, this frame consists of top and bottom rails, two stiles, and a series of drawer rails joined to the stiles with twin mortise-and-tenons. (The bottom rail is joined with blind mortise-and-

tenons.) Apply glue to all the contacting surfaces of the joints and assemble the frame. Install a bar clamp across each of the rails, alternating between the top and bottom of the assembly where possible. To distribute clamping pressure and protect the stock, use two clamping strips. Tighten the clamps a little at a time *(above)*, continuing until glue squeezes out of the joints.

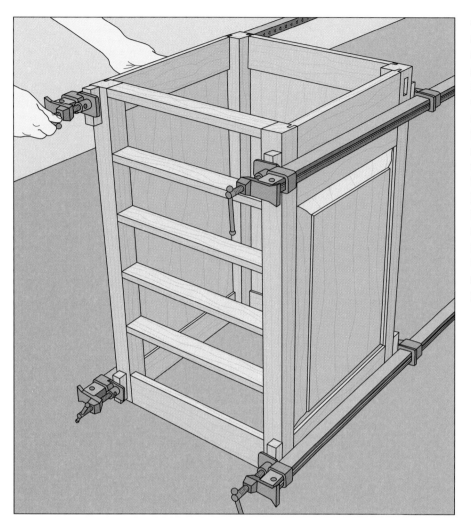

2 Assembling the pedestal

To complete the pedestal, build side assemblies to fit between the front and rear assemblies *(page 47)*. Each side assembly needs only a panel and two rails, since it will share stiles with the front and rear assemblies. For a double-pedestal desk, the top rail of the assembly facing the second pedestal should be wider than the height of the central drawer between the two pedestals *(page 31)*. Once you have prepared all the parts, test-fit them, then sand their inside faces. Apply glue to all the joints—with the exception of the panel grooves—and assemble the pedestal. Clamp the pedestal with bar clamps spanning the side rails *(left)*; use wood pads to protect the stiles.

3 Checking for square

Measure the diagonals between opposite corners of the pedestal immediately after tightening the clamps *(right)*. They should be equal; if not, the pedestal is out-of-square. To correct the problem, install a bar clamp across the longer of the two diagonals. Tighten this clamp a little at a time, measuring as you go until the two diagonals are equal.

INSTALLING THE BOTTOM

1 Installing ledger strips

To install a bottom using ledger strips, cut four 1-inch-square wood strips to fit along the rails at the bottom of the case. The ends of the strips should butt against the stiles. Bore two sets of countersunk holes in each strip: one centered along one edge, for screwing the strip to the rail, and another along an adjacent edge for attaching the bottom panel. Stagger the holes so the fasteners will not contact each other. With the pedestal upside-down, position a ledger strip on the inside surface of a bottom rail about 1 inch from its top edge. Mark the positions of the screw holes with an awl and bore pilot holes. Using clamps to hold the strip in position, screw the strip in place *(right)*. Repeat for the other ledger strips.

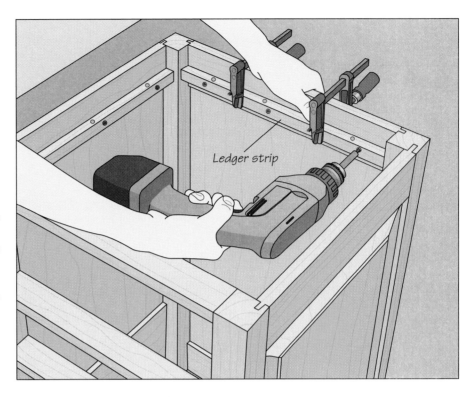

Ledger strip

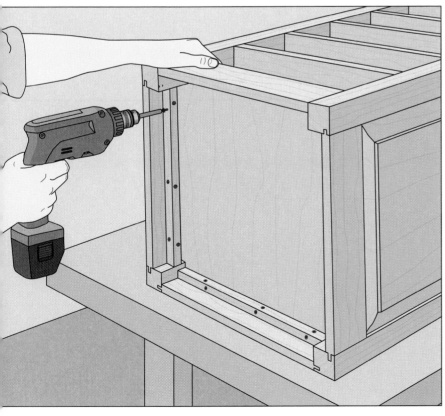

2 Installing the bottom

Cut a bottom panel to fit the case, notching its corners to fit around the stiles. To mount the panel, set the pedestal on its back. Holding the panel flush against the strips with one hand, mark the screw holes with an awl and bore pilot holes. Then screw the bottom in position *(left)*.

JOINING DESK PEDESTALS

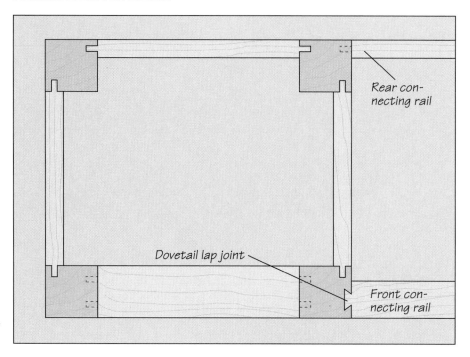

Rear con-
necting rail

Dovetail lap joint

Front con-
necting rail

1 Planning the joinery

Once both desk pedestals are glued up, you are ready to join them. The diagram at left shows the joinery involved. At the back of the desk, a rear connecting rail is attached to the stiles of the pedestals with blind mortise-and-tenons; this rail provides structural support and hides the back of the central drawer. At the front, a connecting rail, which provides support for the top, is joined to the stiles with dovetailed half-lap joints. Directly below this rail is a support board (visible in the illustration below) for the central drawer. It is connected to the stiles with twin mortise-and-tenons.

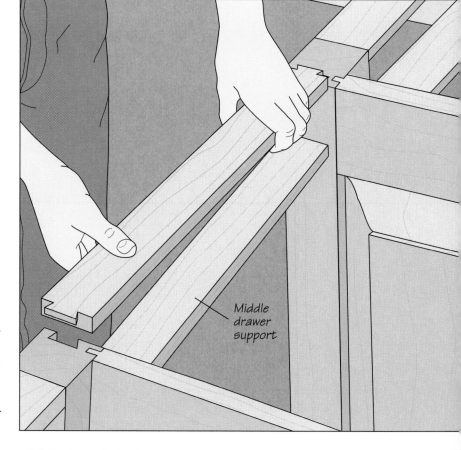

Middle
drawer
support

2 Attaching the connecting rails and drawer support

Test-fit the rear connecting rail and the drawer support in the pedestals. For the front connecting rail, cut a dovetailed half-lap at each end with a dovetail saw *(page 39)*. Use the half-laps to outline the mating mortises at the top ends of the stiles, then cut and chisel them out. Test-fit the rail in the mortises *(right)*, paring the half-laps if necessary to ensure a tight fit.

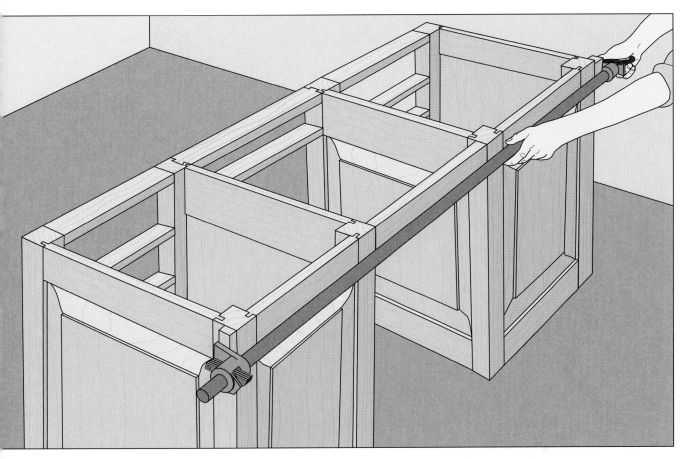

SHOP TIP

Using pipe clamps in pairs

If your pipe clamps are not long enough to glue up a desk, double up two shorter clamps to function as a single unit. To do this, position the two clamps along the desk so the jaws at the handle end grip the desk while the tail stops overlap. Tighten one of the clamps until the tail stops make contact. As you continue tightening, the desk will be pulled together just as if you were using a single long clamp.

3 Gluing up the desk

Apply glue to all the joints between the connecting rails and drawer support and the pedestals and assemble the desk. Clamp the unit across the back with a long pipe clamp *(above)*, using wood pads to protect the stock. Install a second pipe clamp along the drawer support at the front of the desk. Check the opening between the pedestals for square by measuring across the corners. Install a third clamp, if needed.

LEGS AND RAILS

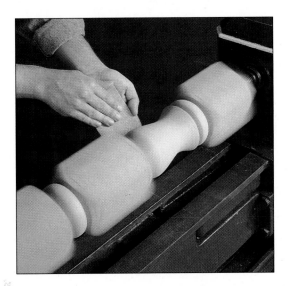

Smoothing a turned leg is simply a matter of leaving it rotating on the lathe and allowing the sandpaper to do its work. The process typically begins with 80-grit paper and works its way up to 180 grit or finer.

Legs and rails are the structural heart of most tables and desks. The furniture legs provide vertical support, and the rails connect and brace the legs while also supporting the top and framing the drawer assembly.

Strength and beauty must be in harmony here: The shape and proportion of the legs and rails must complement other elements of the piece of furniture, balancing the weight of the top and the size of the drawers, for example.

The following chapter demonstrates the techniques for making many of the most common types of table and desk legs, including tapered, cabriole, turned, pedestal, and octagonal pieces. This is followed by detailed instructions for joining legs to rails.

Making the legs is usually the first step in constructing a table or desk. Since most legs require thicker stock than is commonly available, you usually must face-glue thinner stock into a blank of appropriate size *(see front endpaper)*. Make sure the length of the blank is proportional to the intended height of the table or desk, and that it will be strong enough without appearing too bulky. Also consider the design and planned use of the piece before choosing an appropriate leg style.

The delicate cabriole leg *(page 63)* has been a popular feature of high-quality furniture for more than two centuries. Simple to cut on the band saw, the cabriole is designed to suggest the leg of a leaping animal. Tapered legs *(page 60)* can be cut on a jointer or table saw and are suitable for a wide range of tables and desks. They are a simpler alternative to turned legs *(page 66)*.

A table is only as sturdy as the joinery used for the leg-to-rail assembly. Traditional joints, such as the mortise-and-tenon *(page 34)* or dowel joint are reliable. If the piece will be moved frequently, commercial or shop-made hardware *(page 84)* that allows the legs to be removed may be your best option. In designing your table or desk, take into account the method you will use to attach the top to the rails. If, for example, you plan to use wood buttons *(page 98)*, you will need to cut the grooves in the rails before they are fastened to the legs. A lower rail, or stretcher, can be added to any table for extra strength or decorative effect; gate-leg tables may require these bottom rails to serve as anchoring points for any extra legs.

A tusk tenon joint connects the stretcher to the legs of a trestle table. The tenon will extend beyond the through mortise in the leg so that a tusk-like wedge can be inserted to lock the joint while allowing it to be disassembled.

LEG STYLES AND HARDWARE

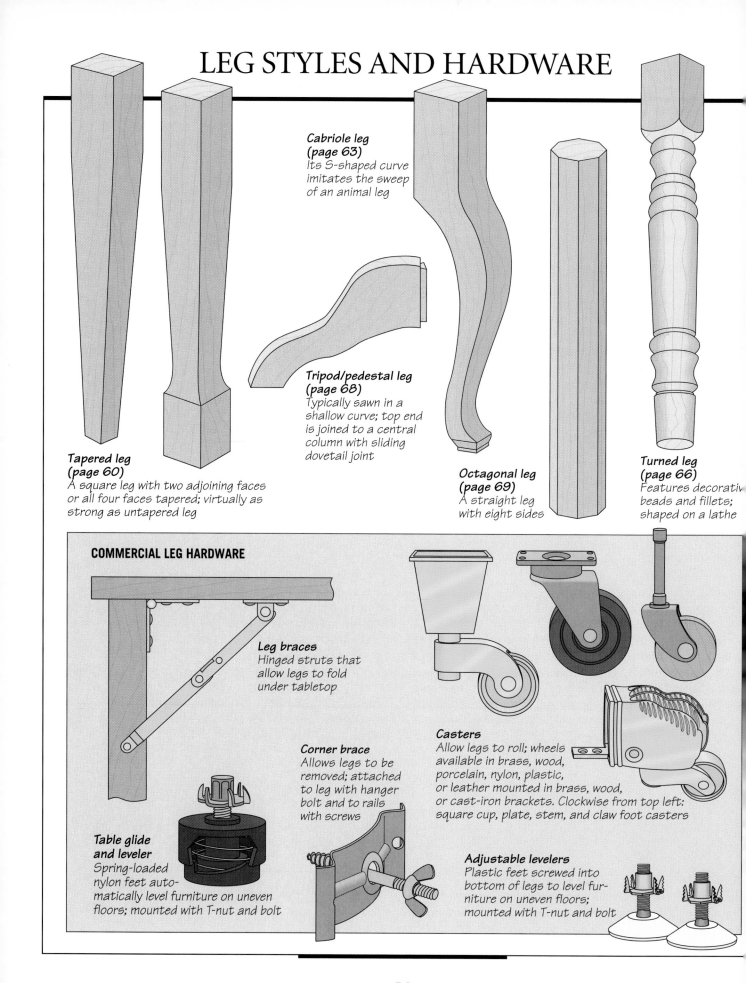

**Cabriole leg
(page 63)**
Its S-shaped curve
imitates the sweep
of an animal leg

**Tripod/pedestal leg
(page 68)**
Typically sawn in a
shallow curve; top end
is joined to a central
column with sliding
dovetail joint

**Tapered leg
(page 60)**
A square leg with two adjoining faces
or all four faces tapered; virtually as
strong as untapered leg

**Octagonal leg
(page 69)**
A straight leg
with eight sides

**Turned leg
(page 66)**
Features decorative
beads and fillets;
shaped on a lathe

COMMERCIAL LEG HARDWARE

Leg braces
Hinged struts that
allow legs to fold
under tabletop

Corner brace
Allows legs to be
removed; attached
to leg with hanger
bolt and to rails
with screws

Casters
Allow legs to roll; wheels
available in brass, wood,
porcelain, nylon, plastic,
or leather mounted in brass, wood,
or cast-iron brackets. Clockwise from top left:
square cup, plate, stem, and claw foot casters

**Table glide
and leveler**
Spring-loaded
nylon feet auto-
matically level furniture on uneven
floors; mounted with T-nut and bolt

Adjustable levelers
Plastic feet screwed into
bottom of legs to level furniture on uneven floors;
mounted with T-nut and bolt

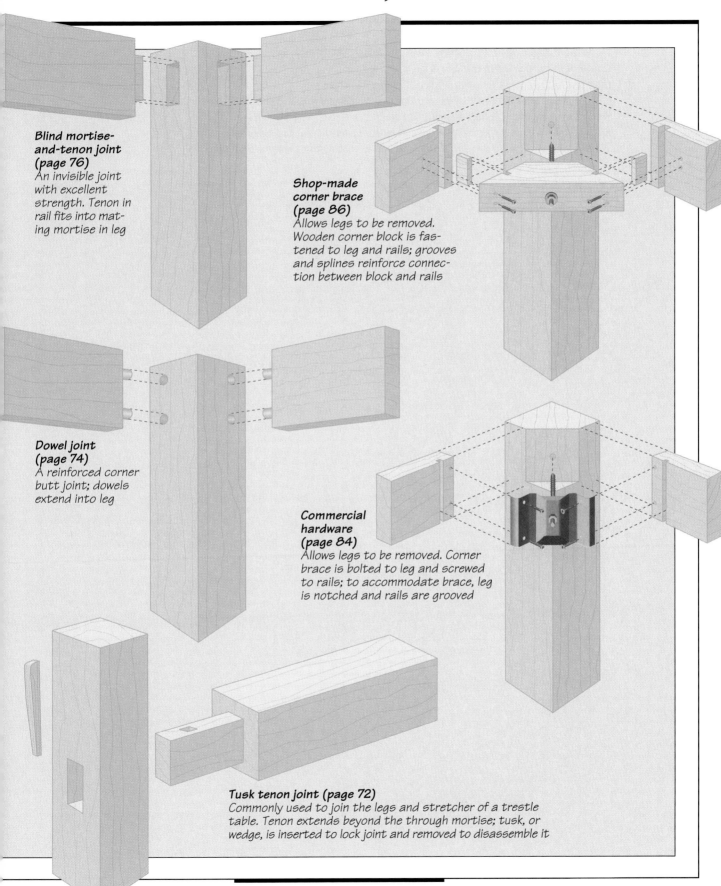

Blind mortise-and-tenon joint (page 76)
An invisible joint with excellent strength. Tenon in rail fits into mating mortise in leg

Shop-made corner brace (page 86)
Allows legs to be removed. Wooden corner block is fastened to leg and rails; grooves and splines reinforce connection between block and rails

Dowel joint (page 74)
A reinforced corner butt joint; dowels extend into leg

Commercial hardware (page 84)
Allows legs to be removed. Corner brace is bolted to leg and screwed to rails; to accommodate brace, leg is notched and rails are grooved

Tusk tenon joint (page 72)
Commonly used to join the legs and stretcher of a trestle table. Tenon extends beyond the through mortise; tusk, or wedge, is inserted to lock joint and removed to disassemble it

TRIPOD TABLE

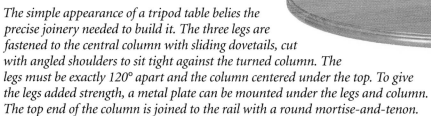

The simple appearance of a tripod table belies the precise joinery needed to build it. The three legs are fastened to the central column with sliding dovetails, cut with angled shoulders to sit tight against the turned column. The legs must be exactly 120° apart and the column centered under the top. To give the legs added strength, a metal plate can be mounted under the legs and column. The top end of the column is joined to the rail with a round mortise-and-tenon.

ANATOMY OF A TRIPOD TABLE

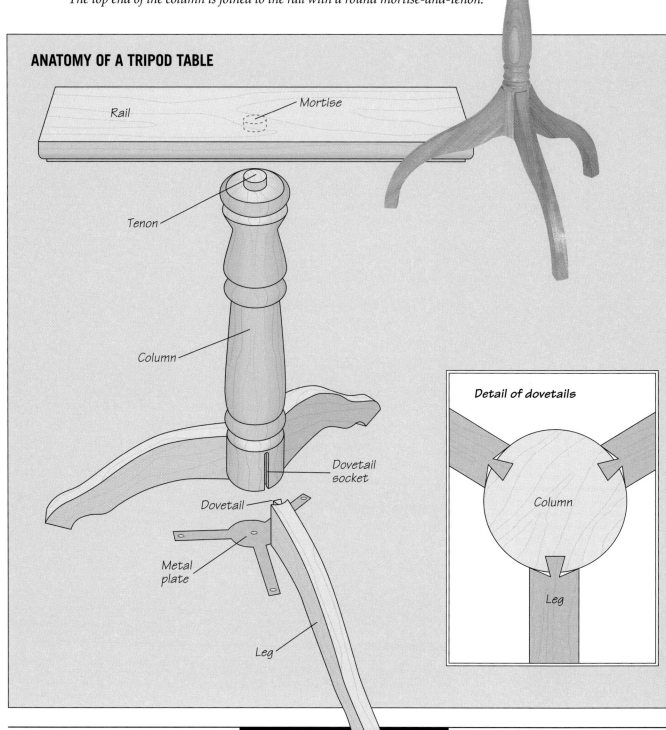

Rail

Mortise

Tenon

Column

Dovetail socket

Dovetail

Metal plate

Leg

Detail of dovetails

Column

Leg

PEDESTAL TABLE

As on the tripod table, the legs of a pedestal table are attached to a central column with sliding dovetails, usually reinforced with a metal plate. The rails are secured to the column with a type of interlocking bridle joint consisting of crossing edge half-laps and mortises. The large table shown at right is supported by two sets of legs and columns. Because of the table's considerable weight, casters have been attached to the legs to make the piece easier to move.

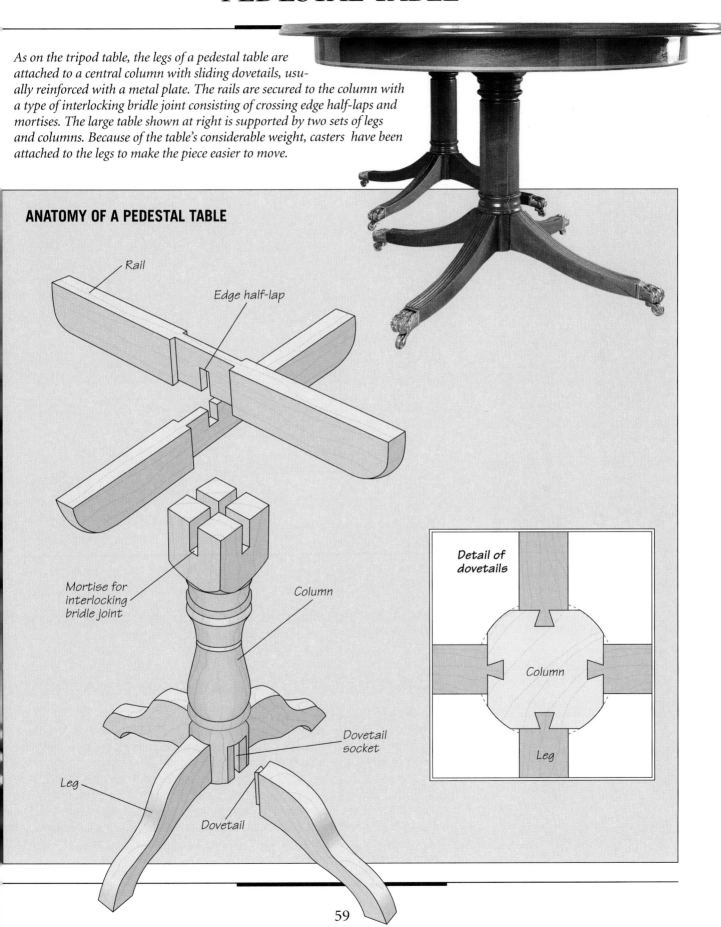

ANATOMY OF A PEDESTAL TABLE

Rail

Edge half-lap

Mortise for interlocking bridle joint

Column

Dovetail socket

Leg

Dovetail

Detail of dovetails

Column

Leg

TAPERED LEGS

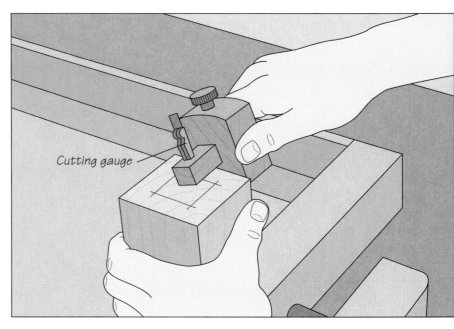

CUTTING A FOUR-SIDED TAPER

Cutting gauge

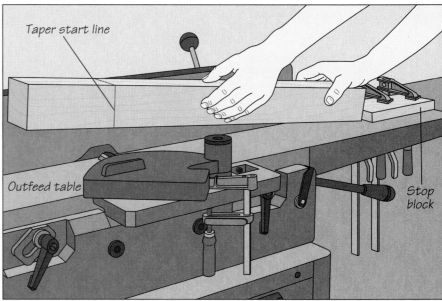

Taper start line

Outfeed table

Stop block

Tapered and stop-tapered legs like those shown above are frequently used on drop-front and rolltop desks and a wide assortment of tables. They lighten a piece's appearance without seriously diminishing its strength.

1 Setting up and starting the cut
You can taper legs quickly and accurately on a jointer. Start by outlining the dimensions of the taper on the bottom of the leg blank with a cutting gauge *(above, top)*. Then mark lines on the four faces of the stock to indicate where the taper will begin. Install a clamp to hold the guard out of the way during the operation. Set the depth of cut for ⅛ inch and, holding the blank against the fence, align the taper start line with the front of the outfeed table. Butt a stop block against the bottom of the leg and clamp it to the infeed table. To start each pass, carefully lower the blank onto the cutterhead while holding it firmly against the fence and the stop block *(above, bottom)*. Make sure both hands are over the infeed side of the table.

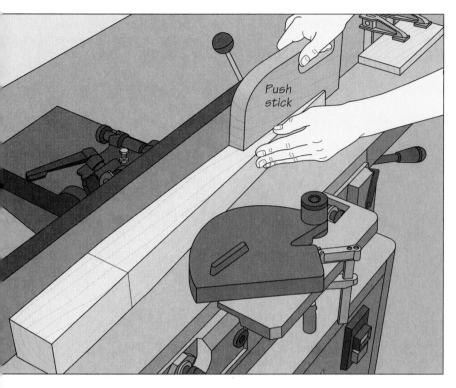

2 Jointing the taper
Feed the leg across the cutterhead with a push stick, pushing down on the trailing end of the stock while pressing it flush against the fence *(left)*. Keep your left hand away from the cutterhead. Make as many passes as necessary until you have trimmed the stock to the taper outline, then repeat the process to shape the remaining faces. Make the same number of passes on each side.

JOINTING A STOPPED TAPER

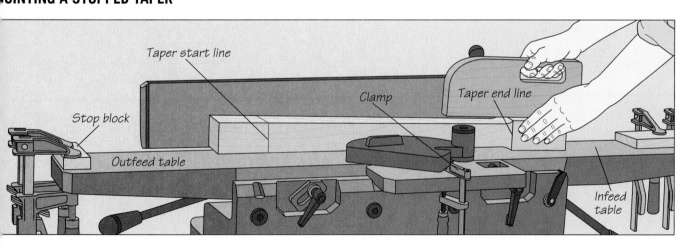

Using twin stop blocks

Mark lines on all faces of the leg blank to indicate where the tapering will begin and end. Install a clamp on your jointer's infeed table to hold the guard out of the way. Set a ⅛-inch depth of cut, then butt the blank against the fence with the taper line about ¾ inch in front of the edge of the outfeed table. (The extra ¼ inch will compensate for the fact that, as the infeed table is lowered later, it will also slide back.) Butt a stop block against the foot of the blank and clamp it to the infeed table. Next align the taper end line with the back end of the infeed table. Butt a

second stop block against the top end of the blank and clamp it to the outfeed table. To make the first pass, lower the workpiece onto the knives, keeping it flush against the fence and stop block on the infeed table. Feed the workpiece using a push stick *(above)*; use your left hand to press the blank against the fence. Keep both hands well clear of the cutterhead. Make one pass on each face, then lower the infeed table ⅛ inch and repeat the process on all four sides. Continue, increasing the cutting depth with each pass until the taper is completed.

BUILD IT YOURSELF

A JIG FOR TWO-SIDED TAPERS

Tapering legs on a table saw can be done easily with the right jig. The one shown below is made from ¾-inch plywood, some solid wood, and two toggle clamps. It is sturdier than many commercial models; the clamps ensure that the stock is held firmly in place while the cut is being made. Refer to the illustration for suggested dimensions.

To assemble the jig, set the saw blade to its maximum cutting height, butt one side of the jig base against the blade, and position the rip fence against the other side of the base. Lower the blade and mark a cutting line for the taper on one side of your leg blank, then set it on the base, aligning the mark with one edge of the jig. Hold the workpiece securely and butt the plywood guide bar against it. Press the lip snugly against the end of the blank. Screw the guide bar to the base and the solid wood shim to the bar, making certain that their edges are aligned. Attach the toggle clamps to the shim. Clamp down to secure the blank to the jig with the taper mark aligned with the edge of the base. Screw the handle to the base at least 6 inches away from the side that will pass by the blade.

To cut the first taper, clamp a featherboard and support board to the saw table, making sure they will not interfere with the blade. (The featherboard should press only on the jig base, not on the workpiece.) Set the blade height and slide the jig and leg blank across the table, making sure that neither hand is in line with the blade *(below)*. To cut the second taper on an adjacent side of the blank, repeat the pass with the two untapered sides of the blank against the jig base and guide bar. **(Caution: Blade guard removed for clarity.)**

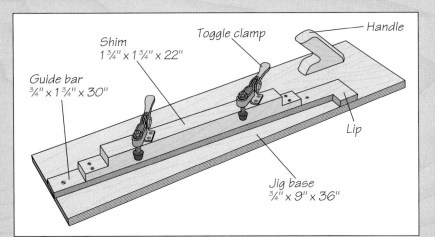

Toggle clamp

Handle

Shim
1 ¾" x 1 ¾" x 22"

Guide bar
¾" x 1 ¾" x 30"

Lip

Jig base
¾" x 9" x 36"

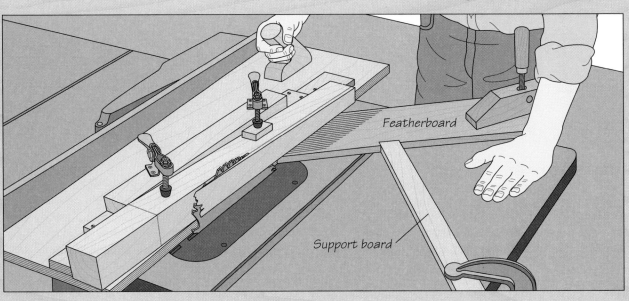

Featherboard

Support board

CABRIOLE LEGS

MAKING A CABRIOLE LEG

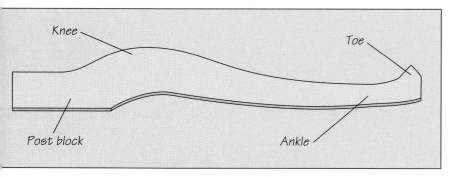

Knee

Toe

Post block

Ankle

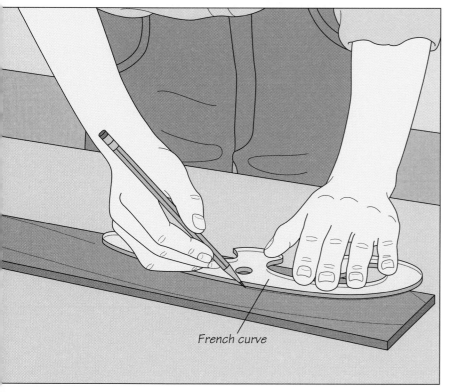

French curve

Designing the leg
For a template, cut a piece of stiff cardboard or hardboard to the same length and width as your leg blanks. The design shown above at top will yield a stable and well-proportioned leg, but you can alter the design to suit your project. Begin drawing the leg by outlining the post block. Make its length equal to the width of the rail that will be attached to it; the post block should be wide enough to accept the rail tenons. Next, sketch the toe and the front of the leg from the toe to the ankle using a French curve *(above, bottom)*; at its narrowest point, the ankle should measure about two-fifths of the stock width. Move on to the knee, sketching a gentle curve from the post block to the front edge of the template about 3 to 4 inches below the block. Then join the knee to the ankle with a relatively straight line. Complete the outline at the back of the leg, connecting the bottom of the leg with the back of the ankle, then sketching a curve from the ankle to the bottom of the post block. You may need to redraw the curves several times until you are satisfied with the design.

Despite its delicate appearance, a cabriole leg provides excellent strength. A well-balanced leg should be able to stand by itself.

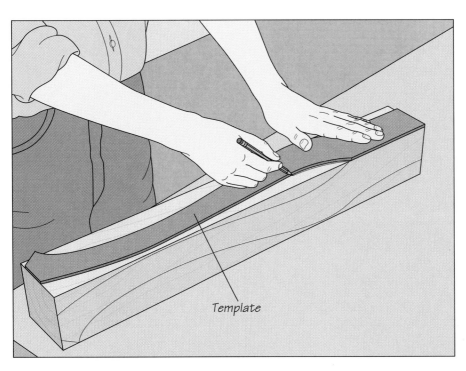

Template

2 Transferring the design

Cut out your template on a band saw, then sand the edges to the marked outline. To trace the outline on the leg blank, place the template flat on one of the inside faces of the blank, making sure that the ends of the template and the blank are aligned and that the back of the post block is flush with the inside edge of the blank. Trace along the edges of the template. Turn the blank over and repeat the procedure on the other inside face *(left)*. At this point, some woodworkers prefer to cut mortises or drill holes for the leg-to-rail joinery. (It is easier to clamp and cut joints on a rectangular leg blank than on a leg with pronounced curves.) Other woodworkers cut the leg first and then do the joinery.

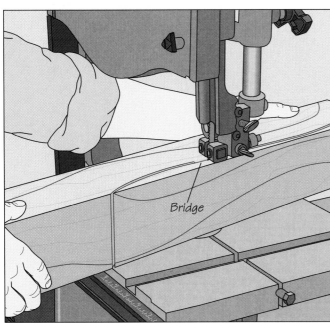

Bridge

3 Cutting out the leg

Set the leg blank on the band saw table with one of the outlines facing up and the toe of the leg pointing away from you. Aligning the saw blade just to the waste side of the marked line for the back of the leg, feed the stock into the cutting edge. Turn off the saw about halfway through the cut and remove the blank. Then cut along the same line from the opposite end. To avoid detaching the waste piece from the blank and losing the marked

outline on the adjacent face, stop the cut about ½ inch from the first kerf, leaving a short bridge between the two cuts *(above, left)*. Retract the workpiece, then cut along the line for the front of the leg, again leaving bridges. Turn the blank and saw along the marked lines on the adjacent side *(above, right)*. This time, complete the cut, letting the waste fall away.

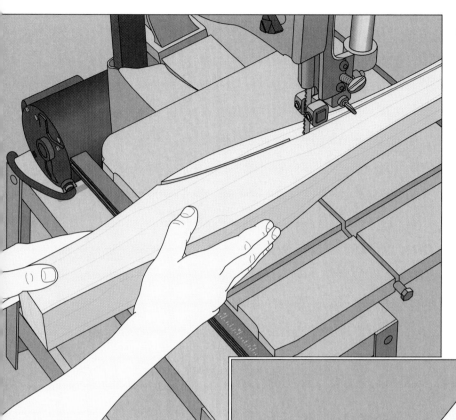

4 Cutting the bridges
Turn off the saw and rotate the blank so that the first side you cut faces up. Slide the blank forward to feed the blade into the kerf at the front of the leg. Turn on the machine and cut through the bridge to release the waste piece. Then cut through the bridge between the kerfs at the back of the leg *(left)*.

Bar clamp

Spokeshave

5 Shaping and smoothing the leg
To finish shaping the cabriole leg and remove blemishes left by the band saw blade, smooth its surfaces with a spokeshave, followed by a rasp and sandpaper. Begin by fixing a bar clamp in your bench vise, then secure the leg in the clamp. Holding a spokeshave with both hands at the top of a curved edge of the leg, pull the tool slowly toward you, cutting with the grain *(right)*. Repeat until the surface is smooth. Turn the leg in the bar clamp to clean up the other edges. Use a rasp to smooth an area that the spokeshave cannot reach. This tool works best when pushed diagonally across the grain. Finish the job with sandpaper, using progressively finer grits until the surface is smooth.

TURNED LEGS

TURNING A LEG

Most turned legs for tables, like the one shown at right, feature a square section, or pommel, at the top. This enables the leg to be joined to the table rails without cutting or attaching hardware to the turned segments.

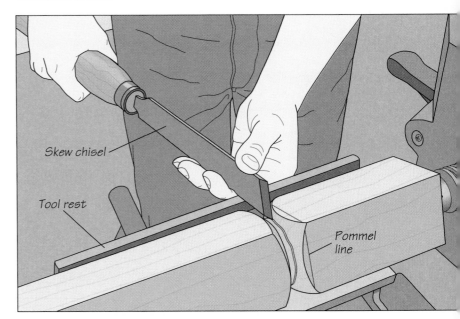

1 Defining the pommel

To turn a leg on a lathe, start by separating the pommel from the cylindrical section. The cylindrical section is then turned *(step 2)* and, finally, the beads and hollows are added *(step 3)*. Begin by marking the pommel on the leg blank, then mount the blank on the lathe and move the tool rest as close to the workpiece as possible without touching it; the pommel should be long enough to accommodate the leg-to-rail joinery method you will use. Next, use a skew chisel to cut a V-shaped notch at the marked pommel line. Bracing the blade against the tool rest, begin with the cutting edge angled slightly to one side so the long point of the tip cuts into the blank. This will define one side of the V. Now, angle the blade to the other side to define the other side of the V notch *(above)*. Continue angling the blade from side to side until you reach the desired depth. As much as possible, keep the bevel of the blade rubbing against the stock at all times.

2 Turning the cylinder

Use a roughing-out gouge to round the corners of the blank below the pommel. With the tip of the gouge tilted up against the rotating blank, gradually raise the handle until the bevel under the tip is rubbing against the stock and the cutting edge is slicing into the wood. Work from below the pommel toward the bottom of the leg *(right)*. Keep the tool at a right angle to the blank throughout the cut. Continue until the blank is cylindrical and smooth.

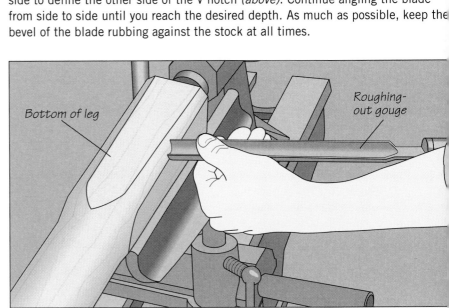

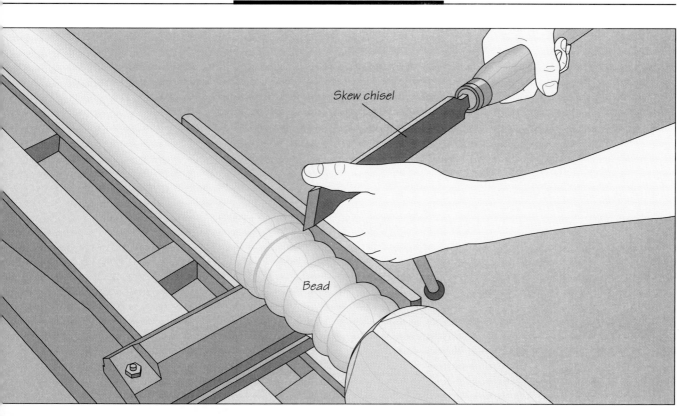

Skew chisel

Bead

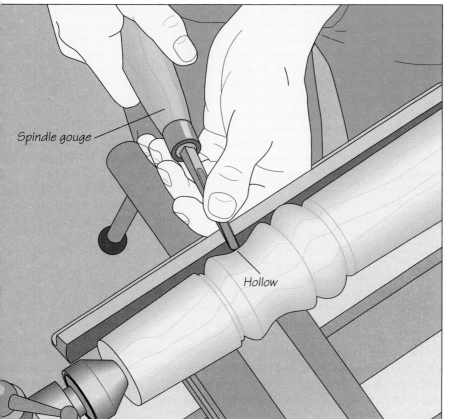

Spindle gouge

Hollow

3 Adding beads and hollows

To form beads, work with a skew chisel and the same technique used to define the pommel. Starting each cut with the tool almost horizontal, raise the handle until the blade slices into the stock. Cut one side of the bead at a time by tilting the cutting edge first to one side and then the other *(above)*. For the hollows, use a spindle gouge. Start each cut at one edge of the hollow with the blade on edge so that its concave side is facing the opposite edge of the hollow. Raise the handle so the tip begins slicing into the stock. Then, sweep the tool toward the hollow's opposite edge, rolling the blade so that, at the center of the hollow, the concave side of the blade is facing up *(left)*. Remove the gouge and repeat the cut from the opposite edge of the hollow, with the concave side of the blade facing toward the hollow. Continue sweeping and rolling the blade from side to side, always working downhill, until the hollow is symmetrical and smooth.

PEDESTAL LEGS

The pedestal, or tripod, leg is best cut on the band saw. The legs have a flat section at the bottom and a dovetail at the top that fits into the central column. Because dovetails are more difficult to cut in a contoured workpiece, it is best to prepare the leg blank for joinery (pages 79 and 82) before shaping it.

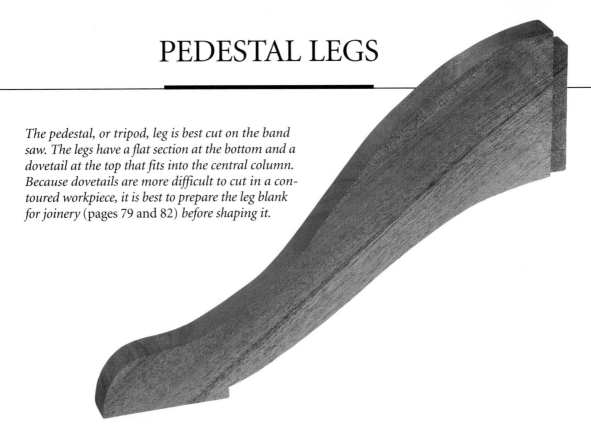

CUTTING A PEDESTAL LEG

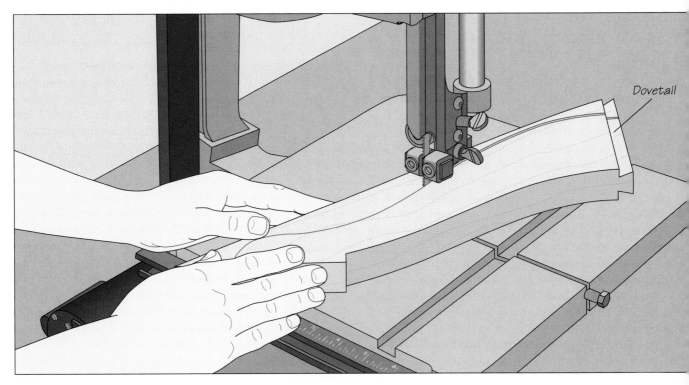

Dovetail

Sawing the leg on the band saw

Cut a dovetail on the top end of your leg blank, using either the table saw *(page 79)* or a router table *(page 82)*. Then, outline the leg on your blank; use a pencil and a French curve as you would for a cabriole leg *(page 63)*. There are three absolute rules for designing a pedestal leg: The grain should follow the slope of the leg, the top and bottom ends must be perpendicular to each other, and the spread of the legs must be less than the diameter of the tabletop. Once you are satisfied with the design, cut the first leg on the band saw *(above)* and use it as a template for the others. Keep a copy of the template for future projects.

OCTAGONAL LEGS

SHAPING AN OCTAGONAL LEG

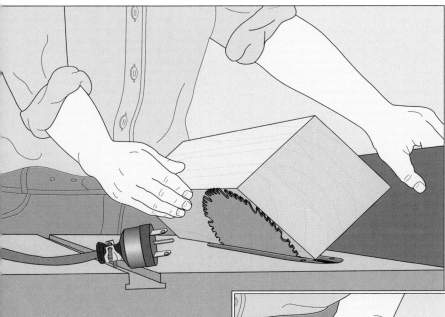

Cutting the leg on the table saw

To set up this operation, unplug the saw, crank the blade to its highest setting, and adjust the cutting angle to 45°. The rip fence should be positioned so that the blade is tilted away from it. Lay one face of the leg blank on the blade with a corner resting on the saw table, then butt the fence against the stock *(above)* and lock it in place. To make the first cut, butt the stock face-down against the rip fence a few inches in front of the blade. Adjust the cutting height until one tooth just protrudes beyond the face of the workpiece. Feed the blank into the blade, straddling the fence with your hand. Rotate the leg 90° clockwise and repeat the cut on the adjacent face. Continue in this manner *(right)* until the sides are cut.

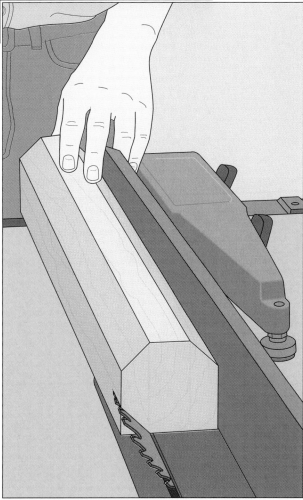

The attractive octagonal leg is simple to cut on the table saw.

Commercial marquetry banding adds a decorative touch to a tapered leg.

CUTTING GROOVES FOR INLAY

Using a table saw

To cut a straight groove for inlay, use a table saw with a dado head the same width as the inlay. If you are working with thick shop-made inlay, set the cutting height to slightly less than the thickness of the inlay; for commercial inlay, set the cutting height to its exact thickness. Make a cut in a scrap board, test the fit, and adjust the width and cutting height of the blades, if necessary. Next, mark a line for the groove on the leading end of the leg and align it with the dado head. Butt the rip fence against the stock, then feed it across the blades *(above)*.

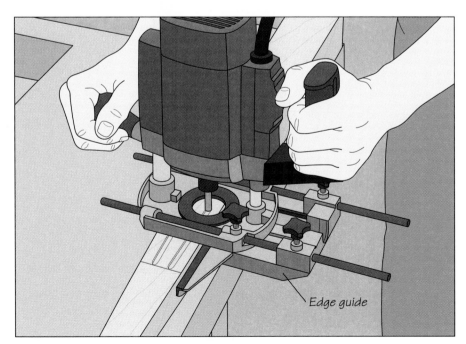

Edge guide

Using a router

To make a groove that requires more than one straight cut at different angles, use a router with a commercial edge guide. Secure the leg to a work surface, then fit the router with a straight bit the same width as the inlay and set the cutting depth. Remember, the groove should be slightly shallow for shop-made inlay, but full-depth for commercial inlay. Outline the groove on the leg, align the bit over one of the lines that run along the grain, and butt the edge guide's fence against the stock. Gripping the router firmly, cut the groove; remember to move the tool against the direction of bit rotation. Repeat to cut the other grooves *(left)*. For the short cuts against the grain, clamp a wooden edge guide across the leg. Finally, square the corners with a chisel.

GLUING DOWN THE INLAY

Setting the inlay in the groove

Cut the inlay to length to fit the groove. If you are using shop-made inlay, use a table saw or a backsaw in a miter box; for commercial inlay, use a wood chisel. To install inlay in the four-sided groove shown, make miter cuts at the ends of the inlay pieces. It is easiest to cut and dry-fit one piece at a time, making sure you align the miter cuts with the corners of the grooves. With commercial inlay marquetry, try to match the pattern at the corners to form one continuous design. Once all the pieces are cut to size, spread a thin layer of glue in the groove and on the mitered ends of the inlay. Insert one strip at a time. While the glue dries, secure the inlay with strips of masking tape.

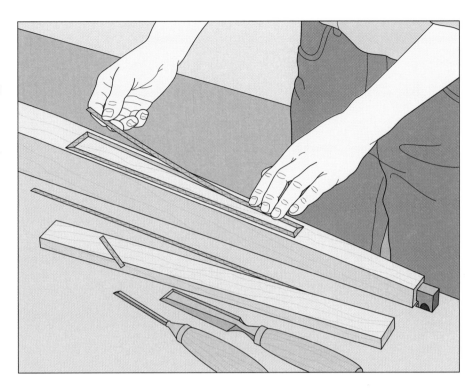

DETAILING A LEG

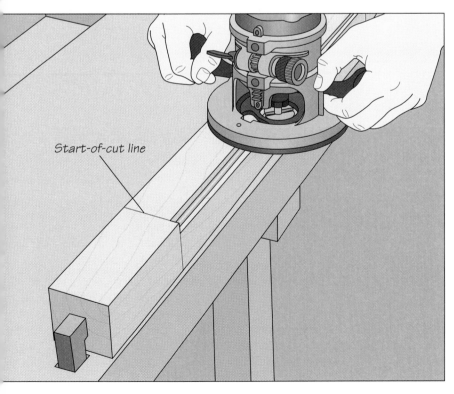

Start-of-cut line

Routing edge detail

Secure the leg to a work surface. Mark lines on the leg for the beginning and end of the cut, then install a decorative bit in your router. A piloted quarter-round bit is shown; this bit will rout a raised bead along the front corners of the leg. Set a cutting depth appropriate to the profile you want to make, then align the bit with the start line. Holding the tool with both hands, guide the bit along the corner of the leg against the direction of bit rotation. Keep the base plate flat on the top surface of the leg and the bit pilot pressed against the stock throughout the operation *(left)*. Stop when you reach the end line, reposition the leg on the work surface, and make a second pass, riding the base plate on the adjacent face of the leg. This is usually done only on the leg's outside corner, but the other corners can also be routed depending on the leg design.

LEG-TO-RAIL JOINERY

TUSK TENON JOINTS

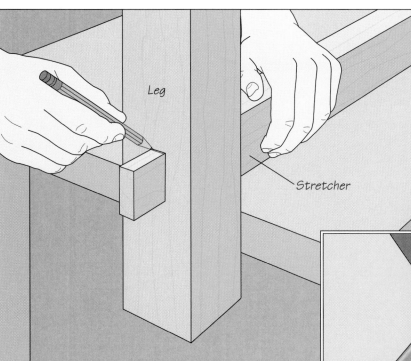

1 Marking the location of the wedge
Cut a four-shouldered tenon *(page 76)* long enough to extend beyond the leg by at least 2 inches; this will provide sufficient stock to resist being split by the wedge. Cut a through mortise to accommodate the tenon and assemble the joint. Then, holding the pieces together on a work surface, mark a line on the top of the cheek where the tenon emerges from the mortise *(left)*.

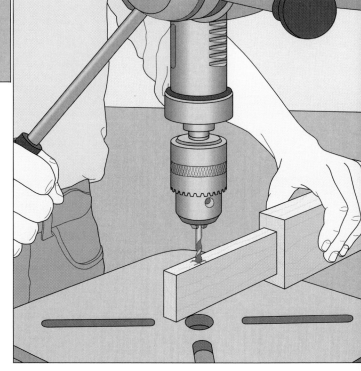

A tusk tenon joins the stretcher to the pedestal leg of the table shown above. Although the tusk joint is assembled without glue so that the table can be disassembled, it is as strong as a glued blind mortise-and-tenon.

2 Drilling the hole for the wedge
Disassemble the joint and make a drilling mark 1/16 inch on the shoulder side of the scribed line; this will ensure a tight fit when the wedge is driven into place. Set a mortise gauge to one-third the thickness of the tenon and use the gauge to outline the hole in the middle third of the top cheek, bordering on your mark. Using a bit slightly smaller in diameter than the outline, bore the hole through the tenon on the drill press *(above)*.

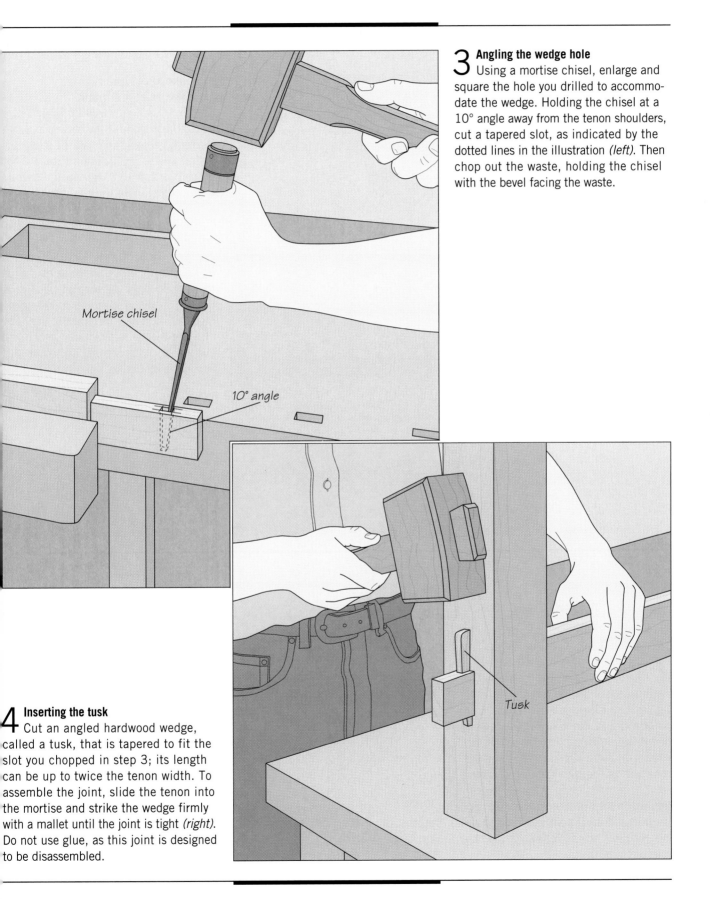

3 Angling the wedge hole
Using a mortise chisel, enlarge and square the hole you drilled to accommodate the wedge. Holding the chisel at a 10° angle away from the tenon shoulders, cut a tapered slot, as indicated by the dotted lines in the illustration *(left)*. Then chop out the waste, holding the chisel with the bevel facing the waste.

Mortise chisel

10° angle

Tusk

4 Inserting the tusk
Cut an angled hardwood wedge, called a tusk, that is tapered to fit the slot you chopped in step 3; its length can be up to twice the tenon width. To assemble the joint, slide the tenon into the mortise and strike the wedge firmly with a mallet until the joint is tight *(right)*. Do not use glue, as this joint is designed to be disassembled.

DOWEL JOINTS

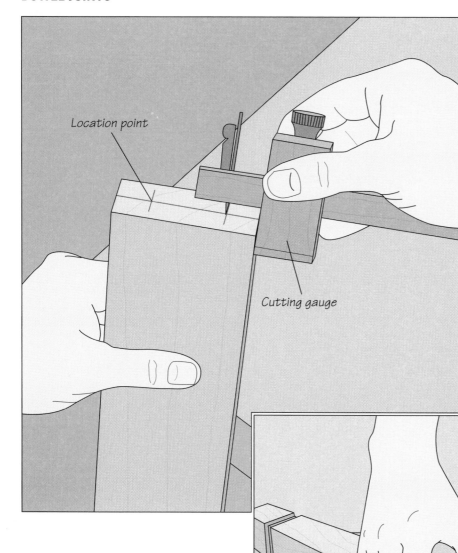

Location point

Cutting gauge

1 Locating and boring dowel holes in the rails

Start by marking the location of the dowel holes. Holding one of the rails end-up, set a cutting gauge to one-half the thickness of the stock and scribe a line across the end of the board. With the gauge at a slightly wider setting, scribe two lines that intersect with the first line on the end of the rail *(left)*. To avoid splitting the stock, use grooved dowels no more than one-half the thickness of the rails. Fit a drill press or an electric drill with a bit the same diameter as the dowels and bore a hole at each location point; the depth should be slightly more than one-half the length of the dowels. Use the same technique to bore the dowel holes at the opposite end of the rail and in the other rails.

2 Pinpointing mating dowel holes

Insert dowel centers in the holes. Then align the top of the rail with the top of the leg *(right)*, and swing the rail up so that its outside face is ¼ to ⅛ inch inside the edge of the leg. A pencil mark like the one shown will help align the rail. Tap the other end of the rail with a wooden mallet. The pointed ends of the dowel centers will punch impressions on the leg, providing starting points for boring the mating dowel holes. Repeat for the other rails and legs.

Dowel center

Alignment mark

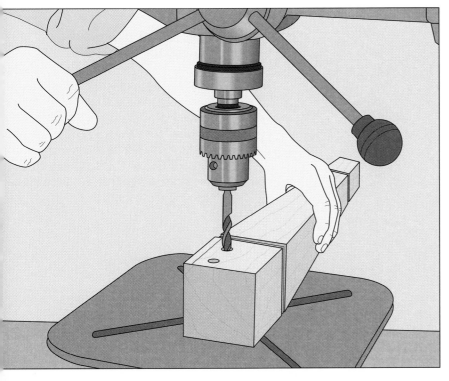

3 Boring the mating dowel holes

Bore the holes in the legs to the same depth as those in the rails—slightly more than one-half the length of the dowels. If you are drilling into a tapered leg on a drill press, be sure to keep the square part of the leg flat on the machine's table.

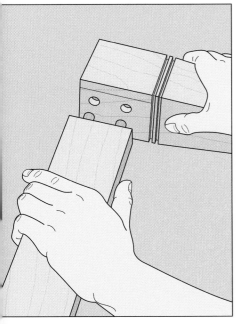

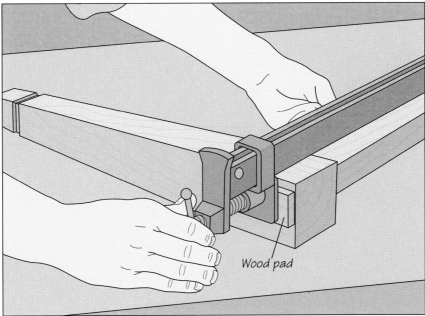

Wood pad

4 Assembling the legs and rails

Spread a little glue on the surfaces of the legs and rails that will contact each other, then dab a small amount of adhesive in the bottom of the dowel holes with a small wood scrap. Avoid spreading glue directly on the dowels; they absorb moisture quickly and will swell, making them difficult to fit into the holes. Insert the dowels into the legs, then tap the rail lightly with a mallet to seat the shoulder. (Be careful about using too much force, which can cause a leg to split.) Fit each end of the rail onto a leg *(above, left)* and hold the joint together with a bar clamp, protecting the legs with wood pads. Align the bar of the clamp with the rail, then tighten it *(above, right)* until a bead of glue squeezes out of the joint.

HAND-CUT BLIND MORTISE-AND-TENONS

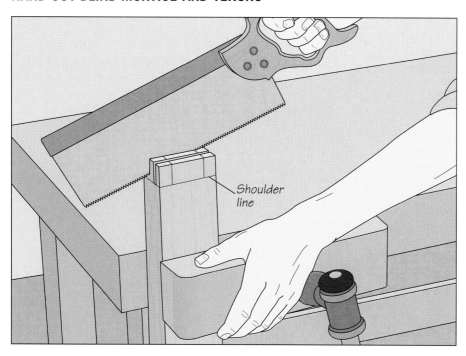

Shoulder line

1 Cutting the tenon cheeks

Outline the tenons on the rails, marking a shoulder line all around the ends so that the length of the tenons will be no more than three-quarters the thickness of the leg. Secure one of the rails end-up in a vise. Cut along the lines on the end of the rail with a backsaw; tilt the saw forward and cut to the shoulder line of the tenon *(left)*. Then complete the cut with the saw level.

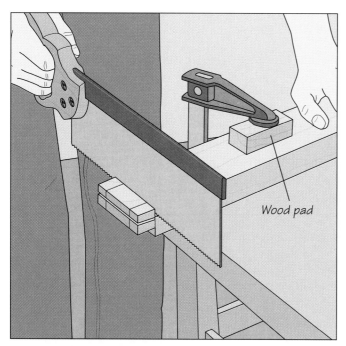

Wood pad

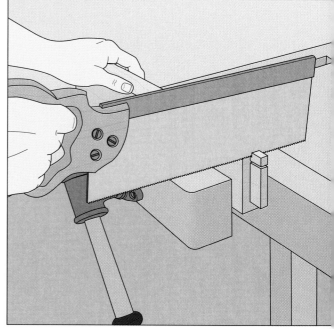

2 Cutting the tenon shoulders

To remove the waste from the tenon cheeks, clamp the rail face-up on a work surface, protecting the stock with a wood pad. Cut along the shoulder line on the face of the rail; turn over the stock and repeat the operation on the other side *(above, left)*. To cut away the waste on the edges of the tenon,

secure the rail end-up in a vise and saw to the shoulder line on both edges of the rail. Finally, clamp the rail edge-up and cut through the shoulder lines on both edges of the rail *(above, right)*. Repeat steps 1 and 2 to cut the tenon on the other end of the rail and at both ends of the remaining rails.

3 Outlining the mortises
Mark the mortise outline on each leg in two steps, using one of the rail tenons as a guide. First, hold the cheek of the tenon flush against the leg, with the top of the rail aligned with the end of the leg. Draw a pencil along the edges of the tenon to outline the length of the mortise, then use a try square to extend the lines across the leg. To mark the width of the mortise, hold the edge of the tenon centered flush against the leg and mark along each cheek (right). With a try square, extend the marks along the leg until the two outlines intersect. Repeat the process on the adjacent face of the leg.

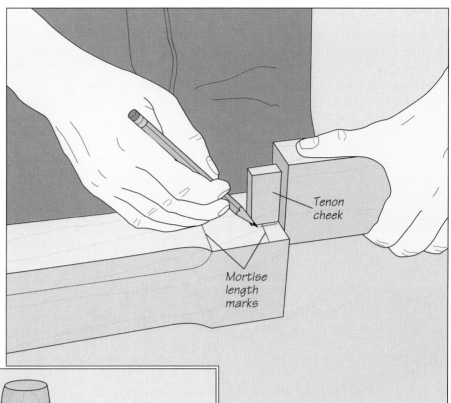

Tenon cheek

Mortise length marks

Mortise chisel

Wood pad

4 Chiseling the mortises
For each mortise, clamp the leg to a work surface, protecting the stock with a wood pad. Then, starting at one end of the outline, hold a mortise chisel square to the face of the leg and strike it with a wooden mallet. Use a chisel the same width as the tenon and be sure that the beveled side of the blade is facing the waste. Make another cut ⅛ inch from the first. Continue until you reach the other end of the outline, levering out the waste to a depth that slightly exceeds the length of the tenon. Test-fit the tenon and widen or deepen the mortise as required. Repeat to cut the remaining mortises. Then spread glue lightly in the mortises and on the cheeks of the tenons. Fit the legs and rails together, then close up the joints with the same clamping setup used for the dowel joint (page 75).

TRIPOD TABLE: ASSEMBLING THE LEGS, COLUMN, AND RAIL

1 Turning the tenon on the column

Start by turning the rail tenon at the top of the column, as shown at right. Then rout the dovetail sockets for the legs at the column's bottom *(step 2)*. Next, cut the dovetails in the legs *(steps 3 and 4)* and assemble the pieces *(step 5)*. Mount the column blank on your lathe and turn it into a cylinder *(page 66)*, leaving a lip and enough stock near the bottom for the leg sockets. To turn the tenon, use a parting tool *(right)*, moving the blade from side to side. The length of the tenon should be about one-half the thickness of the mating rail. Its diameter should be at least ¾ inch and match that of the bit you will use to drill the mortise in the rail.

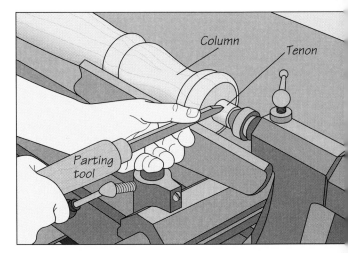

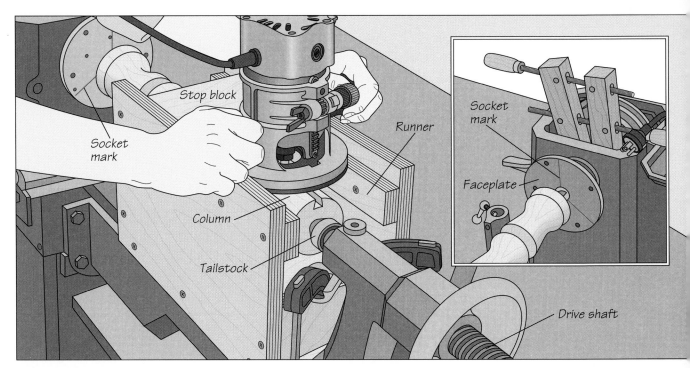

2 Routing the dovetail sockets

Unplug your lathe and turn the column end-for-end to cut the sockets, using a router and a shop-made jig consisting of a ¾-inch plywood box clamped to the lathe bed. Make the box as wide as the router base plate. Attach the two runners so the router bit will cut the sockets with its base plate sitting on them. Next, mark the location of the three sockets on the column; they should be 120° apart. Also mark the upper ends of the sockets, about 3 inches from the bottom of the column. To help align the cuts, transfer the socket marks from the column to the lathe faceplate. Now, rotate the column by hand until one of the marks on the faceplate is vertical and clamp the drive shaft with a handscrew *(inset)*. Cut each socket in two passes, first using a straight bit, then a dovetail bit. Adjust the router's cutting depth, align the bit with the socket end mark, butt a stop block against the router base plate, and screw the block to the jig. Holding the router in both hands, plunge the bit into the column, starting at the bottom, and guide the tool along the runners until the base plate contacts the stop block. Repeat with the dovetail bit *(above)*. To cut the second and third sockets, rotate the column so the socket mark for each cut is vertical.

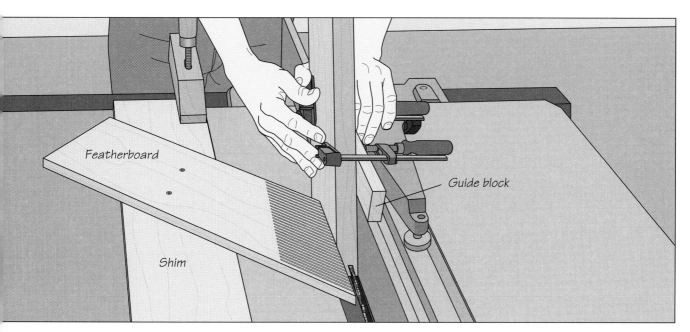

Featherboard

Shim

Guide block

3 Cutting the dovetails

The dovetails in the legs are cut in two steps: The first cut is made on the table saw, and the second by hand. It is easiest to cut the dovetails on leg blanks before shaping the legs *(page 58)*. Adjust your table saw's blade angle to match that of the sockets you cut in step 2. Set the cutting height to slightly less than the depth of the sockets. Outline the dovetails on the edge of one leg blank and, holding the blank on end on the saw table, align a cutting mark with the blade. Butt the rip fence against the stock and lock it in place. Clamp a shimmed featherboard to the table to support the blanks. Also clamp a guide block to the blank; the block will ride along the top of the fence, helping to guide the workpiece. To form the dovetail, make a pass to cut one cheek *(above)*, then rotate the workpiece and feed the opposite face along the fence to saw the other. Once both cheeks of the first dovetail have been cut, check them against a socket in the column. If necessary, adjust the blade angle or height or the cutting width and make another set of passes. Repeat for the other dovetails.

4 Cutting the angled shoulders

The shoulders of the leg dovetails must be cut at an angle so they lie flush against the column. Once the dovetail cheeks are all cut, clamp a blank to a work surface with the cheek cuts extending off the table. Then use a backsaw to cut the shoulders to roughly match the curvature of the column *(left)*. Test-fit the dovetail in its socket and trim the shoulders, if necessary, until you get a suitable fit. Repeat for the remaining dovetails.

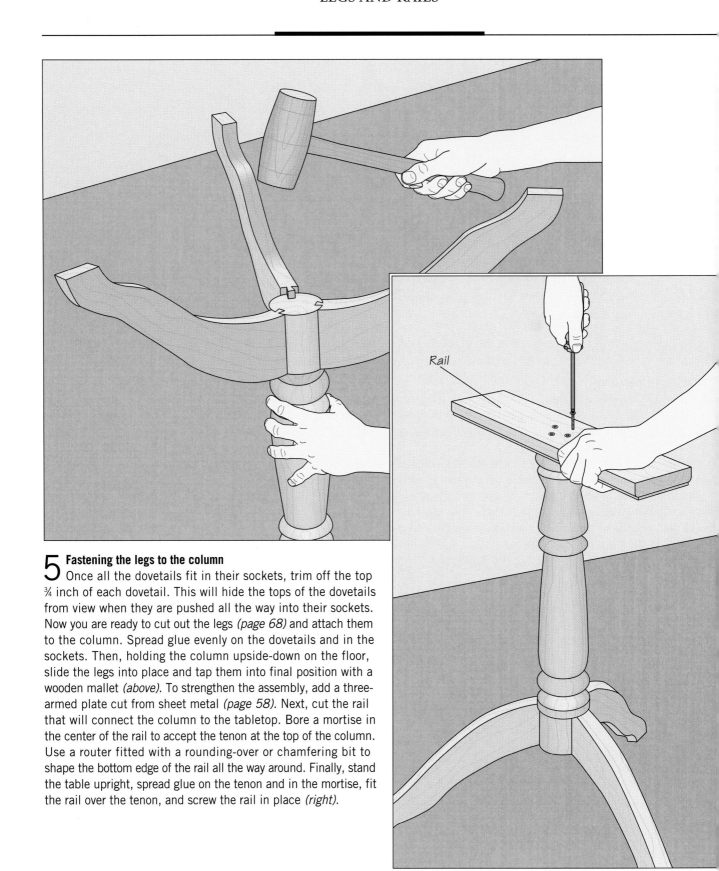

Rail

5 Fastening the legs to the column
Once all the dovetails fit in their sockets, trim off the top
¾ inch of each dovetail. This will hide the tops of the dovetails
from view when they are pushed all the way into their sockets.
Now you are ready to cut out the legs *(page 68)* and attach them
to the column. Spread glue evenly on the dovetails and in the
sockets. Then, holding the column upside-down on the floor,
slide the legs into place and tap them into final position with a
wooden mallet *(above)*. To strengthen the assembly, add a three-
armed plate cut from sheet metal *(page 58)*. Next, cut the rail
that will connect the column to the tabletop. Bore a mortise in
the center of the rail to accept the tenon at the top of the column.
Use a router fitted with a rounding-over or chamfering bit to
shape the bottom edge of the rail all the way around. Finally, stand
the table upright, spread glue on the tenon and in the mortise, fit
the rail over the tenon, and screw the rail in place *(right)*.

EDESTAL TABLE: GLUING UP THE LEG ASSEMBLY

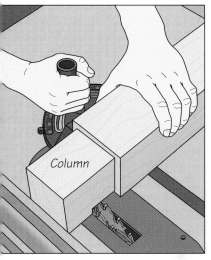

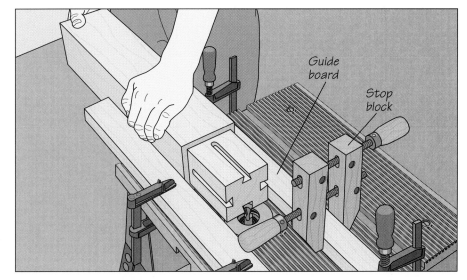

1 Preparing the column for the legs

Mark a line across the column near ne bottom to define the square section nat will be joined to the legs; the area hould be as long as the width of the egs. Install a dado head on your table aw and set the cutting height at rough-▼ ½ inch. Using the miter gauge, make everal passes across the column to emove the waste from all four sides of ne column *(above)*.

2 Cutting the dovetail sockets

Plow a dovetail socket on each side of the column on the router table. Install a straight bit in your router and mount the tool in a table. Mark a line for the sockets down the center of each side, align a socket mark with the bit, butt guide boards against the stock, and clamp the boards to the table. Feed the column across the table to cut the first socket, stopping the cut when the bit reaches the end of the square section. Leave the column in place, turn off the tool, and clamp a handscrew as a stop block against the end of the column. Repeat the cut on the other sides of the column, stopping when the stock contacts the handscrew. Complete the task with a second pass on each side using a dovetail bit *(above)*.

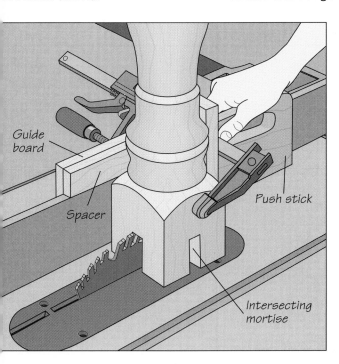

3 Preparing the top of the column

Once the dovetails are cut, turn the column on a lathe, leaving a square section at the top to accommodate the rails and a lip just above the bottom square section to conceal the tops of the legs. (The lip is visible on page 82.) The rails will fit into two intersecting mortises cut in the column's square section. Mark cutting lines for the mortises down the center of each side of the column; the mortise width should be one-half the thickness of the rails. Set the saw blade height to the width of the rails less the edge recess shown in step 7 *(page 83)*. To feed the column safely, make a jig to hold it upright. Take a large push stick and screw a piece of wood to the side, forming an L. With the leg resting snugly in the L, align the cutting mark with the blade and lock the rip fence against the face of the push stick. Lay a spacer on top of the fence (it must be the same thickness as the fence) and screw it to the push stick; screw a guide board to the spacer so the jig forms a channel over the fence. Check the alignment, clamp the leg in place, and make a sequence of cuts until the mortise is wide enough *(left)*. Repeat all cuts on each face to ensure that the mortises are perfectly centered.

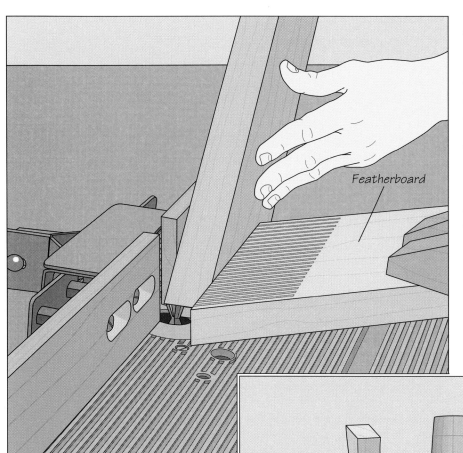

Featherboard

4 Cutting the dovetails on the legs
Install a dovetail bit in your router and mount the tool in a table. Set the cutting depth to make the dovetails slightly shorter than the depth of the dovetail sockets you cut in step 1. Position the fence so that about one-half of the cutter projects beyond its face. With a featherboard clamped to the table to support the workpiece, feed a leg blank *(page 68)* on end across the table pressing it against the fence *(left)*. Turn the blank end-for-end and repeat to complete the dovetail. Test-fit the joint and adjust the fence and make additional cuts, if necessary. Repeat for the other leg blanks.

Lip

5 Joining the legs to the column
Cut out the legs on a band saw *(page 68)*, then notch the top end of the dovetails so that they stop short of the socket end. This will conceal the joints between the legs and column. Spread glue on the dovetails and in the sockets and slide the dovetails into place, tapping them with a mallet if necessary. For additional strength, you can make a four-armed bracket out of sheet metal to fit under the column and legs, and screw it in place, as shown on page 58.

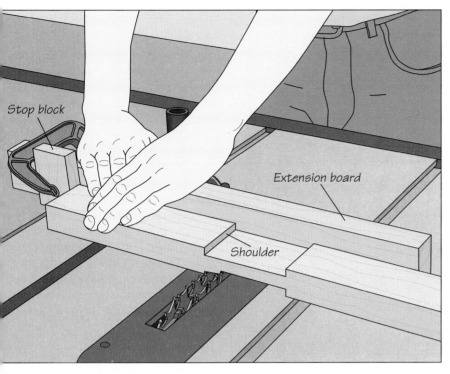

Stop block

Extension board

Shoulder

6 Preparing the rails

To allow the rails to fit the grooves in the column, cut recesses in the middle of both faces of the rails. Install a dado head on your table saw and set the cutting depth to about one-quarter the rail thickness. Screw an extension to the miter gauge. Make test cuts in a piece of scrap to be sure that the rails will fit snugly in the mortises. Mark the shoulders of the recesses on one rail so they are as long as the width of the square section at the top of the column. Align a mark with the dado head and clamp a stop block to the extension, flush against the rail. Feed the rail with the miter gauge, pressing the stock against the stop block. Flip the piece to cut a shoulder on the other face, then rotate the piece and cut the shoulders at the other ends of the recesses. Repeat on the other rail, then remove the stop block and remove the remaining waste.

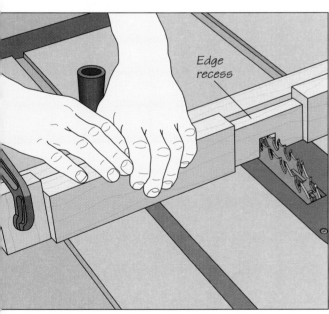

Edge recess

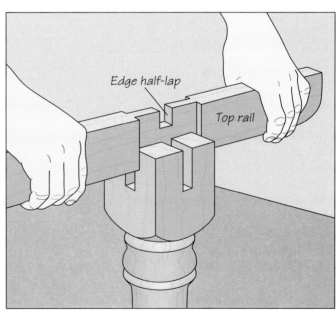

Edge half-lap

Top rail

7 Joining the rails to the column

To conceal the mortises once the rails are in place, cut a ½-inch-deep recess into the bottom edge of each rail, along the length of the recess in the face. Next, notch the middle of the edges. This can be done with the dado head; the width should equal the thickness of the lapped section of the rails. Adjust the blade height to cut halfway through the rail, then saw an edge half-lap in the bottom edge of one rail and the top edge of the other, making sure the notches are centered between the shoulders *(above, left)*. Adjust the blade height for the second rail to account for the edge recess. Once both edge half-laps are cut, round the ends of the rails on the band saw, spread some glue on the contacting surfaces of the column and rails, set the column bottom-end up on the floor, and fit the rails in place *(above, right)*.

COMMERCIAL LEG HARDWARE

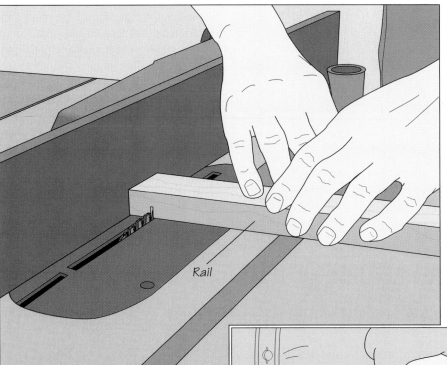

Rail

1 Preparing the rails
Commercial hardware that connects legs and rails should be installed following the manufacturer's instructions. To use the hardware shown on the facing page, test-assemble the leg, rails, and mounting plate, then mark the location of the plate flanges on the rails. To cut the slots for the flanges, align each mark with the blade, then butt the rip fence against the rail. Set the blade height to the length of the flange, adding $\frac{1}{16}$ inch for clearance. Feed the rail into the blade with the miter gauge *(left)*. **(Caution: Blade guard removed for clarity.)** Repeat for the other rail. Slip the flanges into the slots and mark the screw holes on the stock. Bore pilot holes and screw the mounting plate to the rails.

2 Notching the leg for the mounting plate
A notch must be cut at the top of each leg to accommodate the mounting plate. Stand the leg up and hold the rail-and-plate assembly on top of it, aligning the ends of the rails with adjacent sides of the leg. Mark a 45° diagonal line across the top of the leg along the mounting plate. Next, align the top of the plate with the top of the leg and mark a line along the bottom edge of the plate across the inside corner of the leg, adding $\frac{1}{16}$ inch for clearance. To cut the notch, set the leg on a band saw and tilt the table to 45° to align the blade with the diagonal line. Butt a board against the leg and clamp it to the table as a rip fence. Feed the leg into the blade, then clamp a stop block in place to help with repeat cuts *(right)*. Complete the notch using a handsaw.

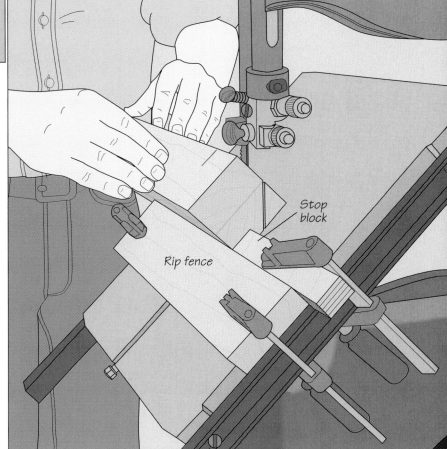

Stop block

Rip fence

3 Preparing the leg for the hanger bolt

Test-assemble the leg and rail-and-plate assembly again and mark the hole on the stock for the hanger bolt provided with the hardware kit. Fit your drill press with a brad-point bit and bore a pilot hole for the bolt using a shop-made V-block jig (*right*). Repeat for the other legs.

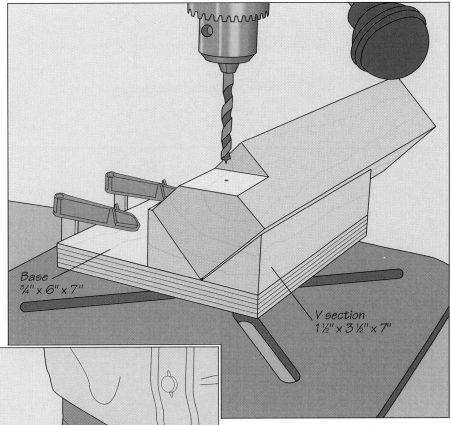

Base
¾" x 6" x 7"

V section
1½" x 3½" x 7"

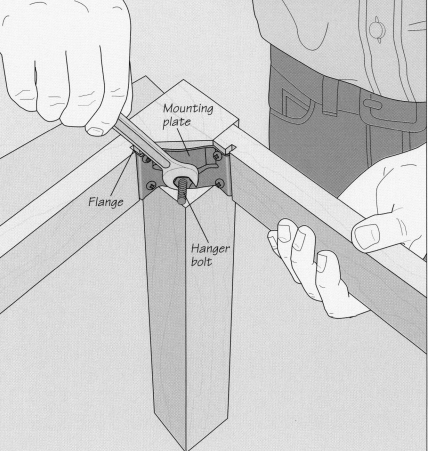

Mounting plate

Flange

Hanger bolt

4 Fastening the leg to the rails

Insert the screw-thread end of the hanger bolt into the pilot hole in the leg. Unlike other fasteners, a hanger bolt has two types of threads: screw threads at one end and machine threads at the other; it also has no head. Screw two nuts onto the machine-thread end and tighten them against each other with two wrenches, forming a temporary head on the bolt. Tighten the bolt with one of the wrenches to drive the screw threads into the leg, then unscrew the nuts from the bolt. Slip the rail-and-plate assembly over the bolt and screw a nut on it. Keeping the top of the rails flush with the top of the leg, tighten the nut (*left*).

BUILD IT YOURSELF

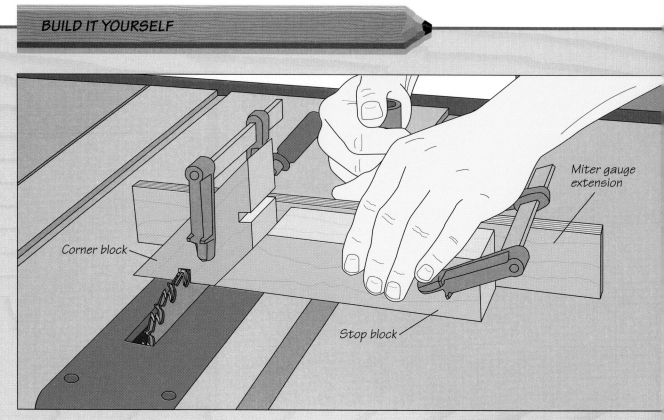

Corner block

Miter gauge extension

Stop block

SHOP-MADE LEG HARDWARE

You can attach a leg to rails using a wooden corner block, a hanger bolt, and four screws. Begin by making the corner block. Cut a piece of wood thin enough to drive a hanger bolt through it into the leg. Then make a 45° miter cut at each end. Next, saw grooves for splines, which will help join the block to the rails. Install a dado head on your table saw with a width and cutting height equal to one-third the thickness of the rails. Screw a board to the miter gauge as an extension, then align the midpoint of one end of the block with the blade. Clamp the block to the extension. Butt a waste piece from the miter cuts against the workpiece to serve as a stop block and clamp it to the extension. Feed the stock into the blades, then turn it over and cut a groove in the other end *(above)*.

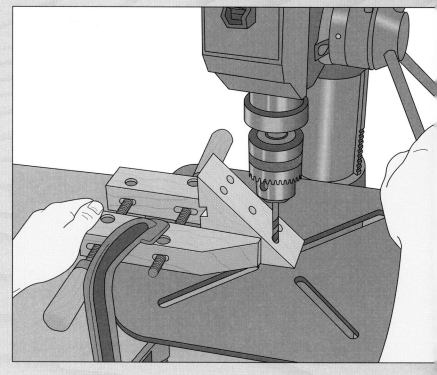

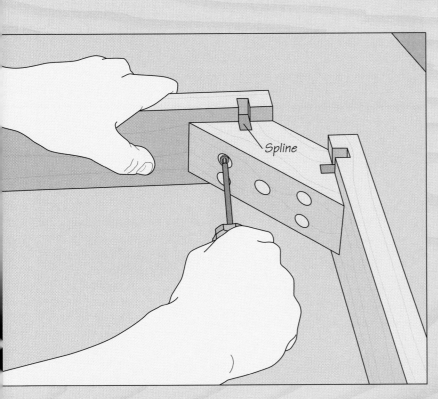

Spline

Next, mark two holes on each side of the clearance hole and drill countersinking holes *(facing page, bottom)*, then install a smaller bit to drill clearance holes for the screw shanks.

To join the leg and rails, first fasten the corner block to the rails. Spread some glue in the grooves in the block and the rails, and insert the splines into the grooves in the block. Then hold the block against the rails and screw it in place *(left)*. Prepare the leg as you would for commercial hardware *(page 84)*, cutting a notch out of the top for the corner block and boring a pilot hole for a hanger bolt. Fasten the leg to the rails with the bolt, slipping a washer between the nut and the corner block. Tighten the nut *(below)* until the leg and rails fit snugly together.

Test-fit the block against the rails, then mark and cut the grooves in the rails. Now cut the splines, making them 1/16 inch shorter than the combined depth of the two grooves. Plane the splines carefully to make sure that they fit precisely in the matching grooves. For maximum strength, make sure that the grain of the splines runs across their width, rather than along their length.

Now bore countersinking and clearance holes for the hanger bolt and screws that will secure the brace to the leg and rails. Install a brad-point bit in your drill press and mark the center of the long edge of the block for a hanger bolt. Secure the workpiece in a handscrew and clamp it to the drill press table, with the center aligned with the bit. Then bore the hole.

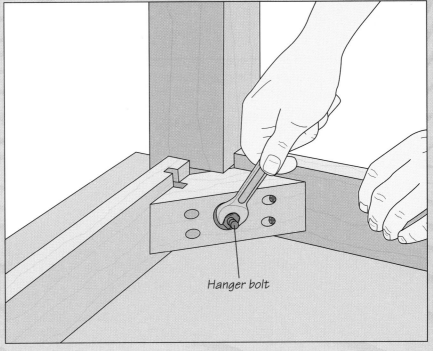

Hanger bolt

TOPS

The top is the reason for a table's or desk's being. The structural requirements are simple: the surface must be flat and solid. The esthetic demands are more complex. The top must complement the design of the table or desk so that it seems to grow out of the assembly supporting it. Since most tops are made of glued-up pieces of solid stock, the grain pattern of the individual boards must be chosen carefully to create the illusion that the surface is made from a single wide board. To do this, you will need to experiment until you succeed. Take your time: Four or five planks, for example, can be flipped and turned end-for-end to create literally scores of possible combinations.

During the Middle Ages, when dining took place in great communal halls, huge trestle tables were the norm: Dozens of people could be fed and the tables could be knocked down for storage after dinner. As separate rooms for public and private dining came into vogue in the 15th Century, smaller, adjustable tables with hinged flaps evolved. These so-called drop-leaf tables were used in coffeehouses and taverns. Other modifications included tables that could split in two to make room for

An adjustable top makes a table more flexible; by mounting sliding table extenders under a table with a divided top, you can expand the table to make room for additional leaves.

additional segments; these were the "draw top" tables popular in Tudor England, and what have come to be known as extension tables. In the early 18th Century, country homes were increasingly furnished with larger drop-leaf tables featuring swinging gate legs.

All the tables and desks built today can be traced to these basic innovations. The following chapter explains how to build and install a variety of tops for tables and desks, from gluing up the top *(page 93)* to attaching it to a base *(page 96)*. While you can make a tabletop by veneering sheet products such as plywood, solid wood remains the building material of choice; sheet materials require edge banding and are often not as appealing visually as solid wood.

The type of top you build depends on the function of your table. If your goal is to maximize seating while reducing storage space, adjustable tops *(page 101)* for drop-leaf, gateleg, or extension tables are a good idea. If you want to add an unusual touch, the section on decorative elements *(page 112)* shows you how to combine wood with such contrasting elements as glass, leather, slate, and felt.

The edge of a tabletop is just as important to its appearance as the wood's grain and color. At left, a router fitted with a rounding-over bit is used to soften the square edges of a mahogany tabletop.

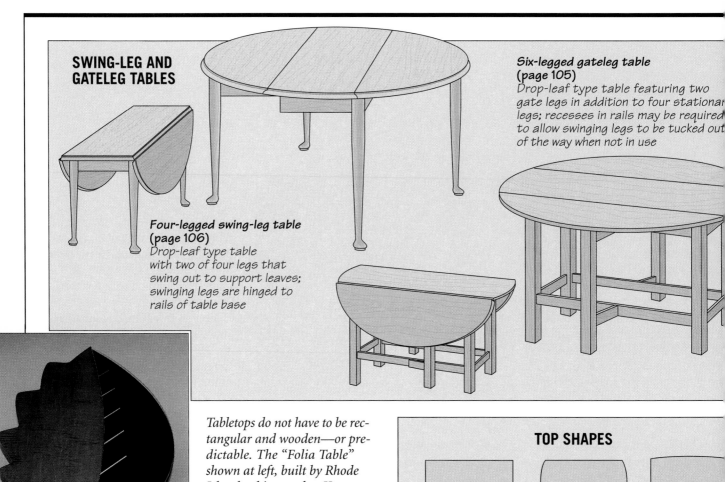

SWING-LEG AND GATELEG TABLES

Six-legged gateleg table (page 105)
Drop-leaf type table featuring two gate legs in addition to four stationary legs; recesses in rails may be required to allow swinging legs to be tucked out of the way when not in use

Four-legged swing-leg table (page 106)
Drop-leaf type table with two of four legs that swing out to support leaves; swinging legs are hinged to rails of table base

Tabletops do not have to be rectangular and wooden—or predictable. The "Folia Table" shown at left, built by Rhode Island cabinetmaker Kam Ghaffari, features a curly maple tabletop dyed black and green, and cut into a stylistic representation of a leaf. The black half of the leaf is lower than the green half; it is covered by a pane of cut glass that rests on stainless steel "veins."

TOP SHAPES

Rectangular

Rounded ends

Curved sides

Rounded ends and curved sides

Round

Oval

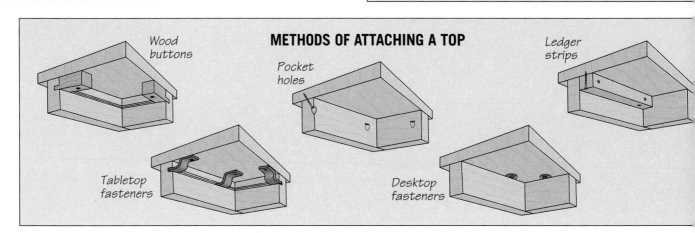

METHODS OF ATTACHING A TOP

Wood buttons

Pocket holes

Ledger strips

Tabletop fasteners

Desktop fasteners

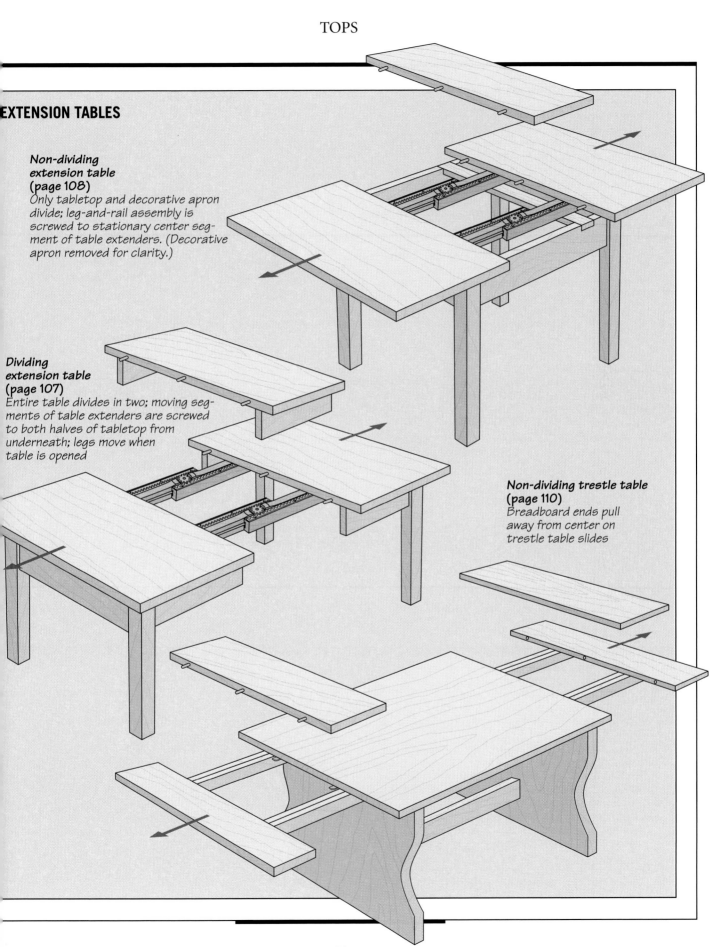

EXTENSION TABLES

**Non-dividing
extension table
(page 108)**
Only tabletop and decorative apron
divide; leg-and-rail assembly is
screwed to stationary center segment of table extenders. (Decorative
apron removed for clarity.)

**Dividing
extension table
(page 107)**
Entire table divides in two; moving segments of table extenders are screwed
to both halves of tabletop from
underneath; legs move when
table is opened

**Non-dividing trestle table
(page 110)**
Breadboard ends pull
away from center on
trestle table slides

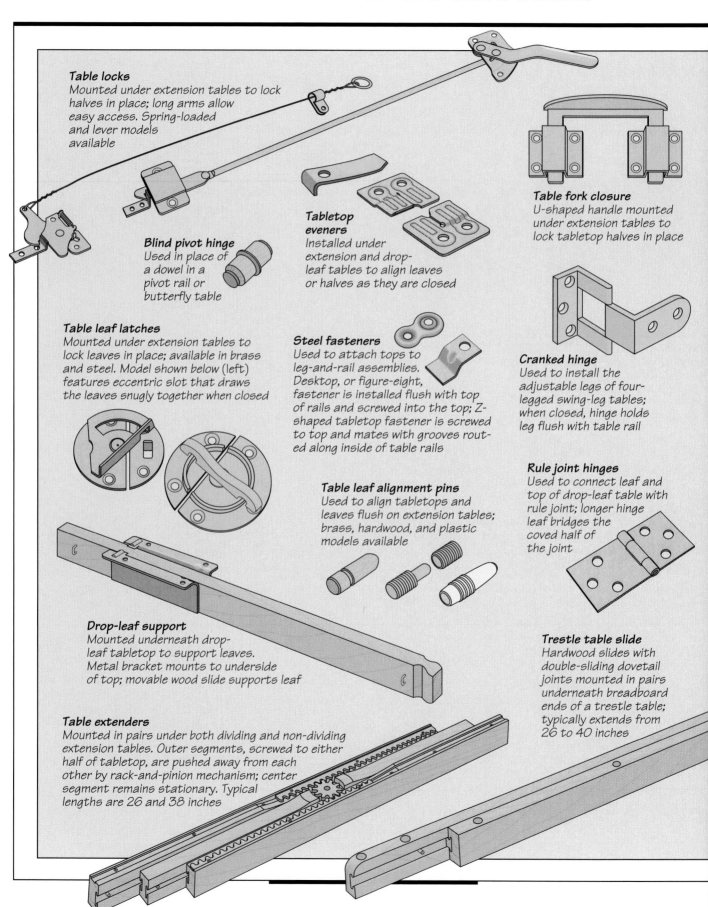

Table locks
Mounted under extension tables to lock halves in place; long arms allow easy access. Spring-loaded and lever models available

Blind pivot hinge
Used in place of a dowel in a pivot rail or butterfly table

Tabletop eveners
Installed under extension and drop-leaf tables to align leaves or halves as they are closed

Table fork closure
U-shaped handle mounted under extension tables to lock tabletop halves in place

Table leaf latches
Mounted under extension tables to lock leaves in place; available in brass and steel. Model shown below (left) features eccentric slot that draws the leaves snugly together when closed

Steel fasteners
Used to attach tops to leg-and-rail assemblies. Desktop, or figure-eight, fastener is installed flush with top of rails and screwed into the top; Z-shaped tabletop fastener is screwed to top and mates with grooves routed along inside of table rails

Cranked hinge
Used to install the adjustable legs of four-legged swing-leg tables; when closed, hinge holds leg flush with table rail

Table leaf alignment pins
Used to align tabletops and leaves flush on extension tables; brass, hardwood, and plastic models available

Rule joint hinges
Used to connect leaf and top of drop-leaf table with rule joint; longer hinge leaf bridges the coved half of the joint

Drop-leaf support
Mounted underneath drop-leaf tabletop to support leaves. Metal bracket mounts to underside of top; movable wood slide supports leaf

Trestle table slide
Hardwood slides with double-sliding dovetail joints mounted in pairs underneath breadboard ends of a trestle table; typically extends from 26 to 40 inches

Table extenders
Mounted in pairs under both dividing and non-dividing extension tables. Outer segments, screwed to either half of tabletop, are pushed away from each other by rack-and-pinion mechanism; center segment remains stationary. Typical lengths are 26 and 38 inches

PREPARING A TOP

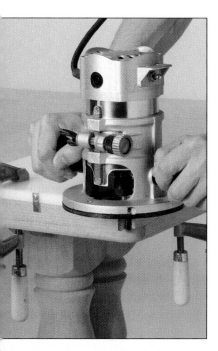

The edges of a rectangular desktop or tabletop are often shaped to soften its contours. Here a router is used with a commercial jig to round the corners of a tabletop. For a gallery of top shapes, see page 90.

Most tops for tables and desks are made by edge-gluing boards together. Few boards are available that are wide enough and most of those would be unsuitable, because of the tendency of wide planks to twist and cup. However, by selecting boards carefully and matching them for color and grain direction, you can create the illusion of a single piece of wood. Assess the color and grain of lumber by planing the surface lightly to reveal what lies underneath a plank's rough exterior.

A sturdy, flat top starts with proper preparation of stock. Make sure you use kiln-dried wood or wood that has been stored long enough in the shop to have a moisture content between 8 and 12 percent. A low moisture content means that the wood will be relatively stable. Also steer clear of bowed or twisted boards. Since many tops have a finished thickness of ¾ inch, 4/4 rough-sawn stock is an ideal choice as it allows you to plane and sand off up to ¼ inch of wood.

Wide tops are seldom glued up all at once because it is much easier to thick-ness plane several smaller panels than one large one. The glue up sequence you follow for your projects will depend on the finished width of your top, and the size of your planer. For example, if you own a 12-inch planer and want a 30-inch-wide tabletop, it is best to glue up three 8- to 12-inch-wide panels and plane them individually, before gluing them into a single top. To help keep the boards aligned during glue-up, some wood-workers use dowels or biscuits spaced every 6 to 8 inches, although this is not essential. Unlike standard tables, the grain for tops for extension tables should be perpendicular to the table's length. Ideally, use quartersawn stock for these tops, as well as for the leaves.

After the glue has dried and the panel has been planed, the edges of the top can be shaped *(page 95)*. With drop-leaf and gateleg tables, this shaping is done before the joinery. One exception is the round drop-leaf table; its leaves should be installed *(page 101)* before the circle is cut to ensure that the table will be perfectly round.

MAKING A TOP

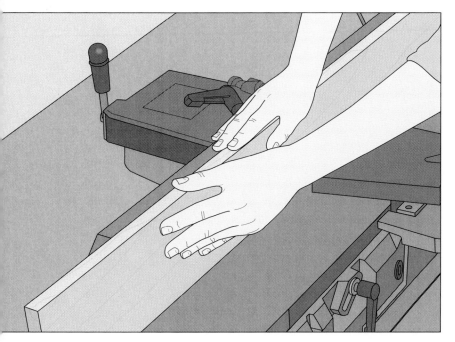

1 Jointing the boards
Prepare each board by first jointing a face and an edge, then plane the other face. Next, roughly crosscut the boards, leaving them about 1 inch longer than the top's final length. Rip the stock so that the combined width of all the boards is rough-ly 1 inch wider than the finished top, then joint all the cut edges *(left)*. Next, arrange the boards for appearance, taking into consideration any leaves if you are making an extension, drop-leaf, or gateleg table. (Leaves are typically glued up separately from the tabletop.) To minimize warping, arrange the planks so the end grain of adjacent boards runs in opposite directions. When you are satisfied with the arrangement, use a pencil or chalk to mark a reference triangle on top of the boards. This will help you correctly realign them for glue-up.

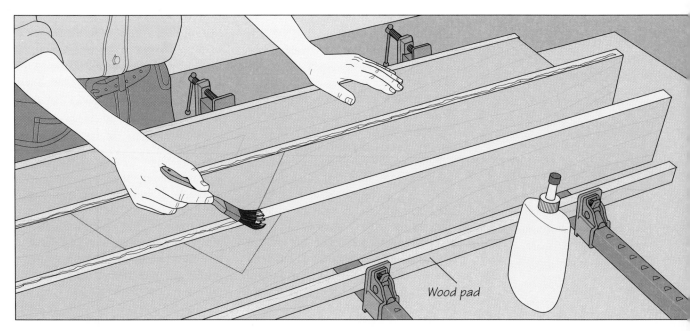

Wood pad

2 Applying the glue

To hold your bar clamps upright during glue-up, cut notched wood blocks and set the clamps in the blocks. Space the clamps at least every 24 to 36 inches. To avoid marring the edges of the panel when you tighten the clamps, cut two wood pads as long and as thick as the boards being glued. Apply a narrow bead of glue to one edge of each joint and use a small, stiff-bristled brush to spread the adhesive evenly on the board edges (*above*). Move quickly to step 3 before the glue begins to set.

3 Tightening the clamps

Lay the boards face-down on the bar clamps and align their ends, making sure the sides of the reference triangle are lined up. Tighten the clamps under the boards just enough to butt them together. To balance the clamping pressure and keep the panel flat, place bar clamps across the top of the panel between the ones underneath. Finish tightening all the clamps in turn (*right*) until there are no gaps between the boards and a thin, even bead of glue squeezes out of the joints. Remove excess glue with a scraper or a damp cloth.

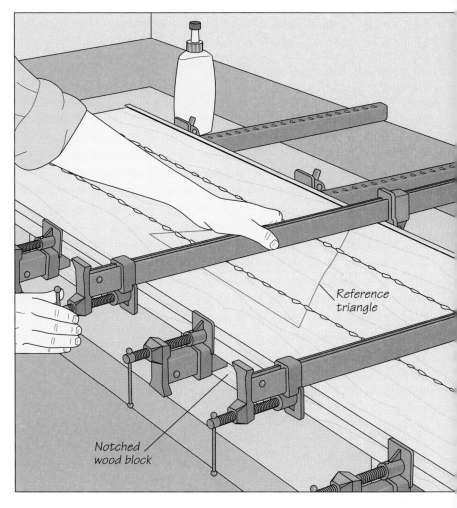

Reference triangle

Notched wood block

SIZING A TOP

Cutting a rectangular top

Once the top has been glued up, rip it to width and trim it to final length. If the top is too large to cut on your table saw, use a router fitted with a straight bit. First, secure the top on a broad work surface and cut it roughly using a circular saw, leaving about ⅛ inch to trim on all sides. Clamp an edge guide to the tabletop near one side so that the router will remove about one-half the waste with the first pass; reset the depth of cut to trim the rest of the waste *(right)*. Repeat for the other edges.

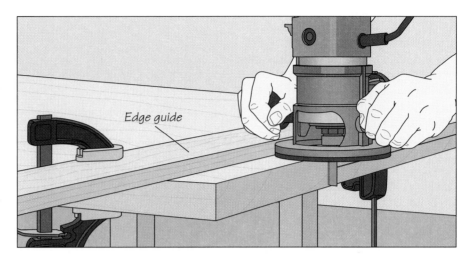

Edge guide

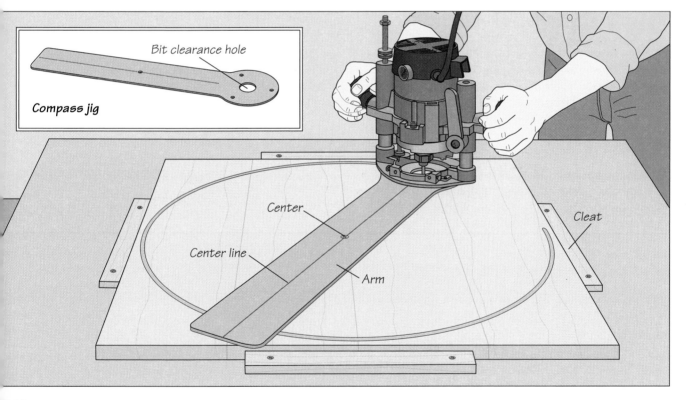

Bit clearance hole

Compass jig

Center

Center line

Arm

Cleat

Making a round top

Scribe a circle on the glued-up top and make the cut with a router. For small-diameter tops, you can use a commercial compass jig; to cut larger tops, use the shop-built compass jig shown in the inset. Make the device from ¼-inch hardboard, sizing it to suit your router. Cut the router end of the jig to the size and shape of your tool's base plate, and make the arm at least 2 inches wide and longer than the radius of the circle you will be cutting. Bore a clearance hole for the bit in the center of the router end, and fix the tool to the jig. Draw a line down the center of the jig arm and mark the radius of the tabletop on it, measuring from the edge of the bit. Drill a hole at this center mark and screw the jig to the center of the workpiece. Secure the stock to a work surface with cleats and a scrap board underneath. Plunge the bit into the stock and rout the circle in a clockwise direction *(above)*. Make the cut in two or more passes, increasing the depth of cut between each pass.

ATTACHING A TOP

Attaching a top to a table or desk is a straightforward task—so long as you consider wood movement. Screwing a top in place without providing for the swelling and shrinking that occurs with humidity changes will result in split or cracked wood. Because wood expands along the grain much less than it does across it, most tops are made with the planks running lengthwise. One exception to this rule is extension tables, where the grain must be aligned across the width of the table so that the two halves do not expand in width at different rates, causing the slides to bind.

Several popular methods for securing tops to tables and desks are shown in this section, including screwing the rails to the top *(see below)* and using wood buttons *(page 98)*, ledger strips *(page 97)*, screws in pocket holes *(page 98)*, and steel desktop fasteners *(page 100)*. For each of these methods, the rails of the leg-and-rail assembly need to be prepared for the top before the legs and rails can be glued up.

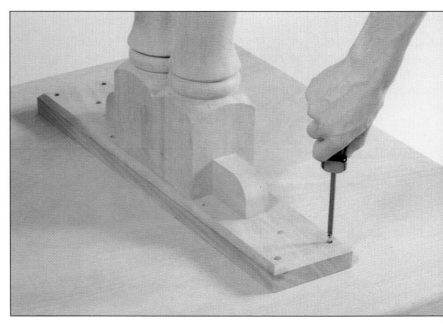

Trestle tables are often designed to be disassembled. In the example shown above, the screws attaching the base of the table to the top can easily be removed. The countersunk screw holes are elongated to allow for wood movement across the grain.

SCREWING THE RAIL TO THE TOP

1 Drilling the holes
To attach a tabletop or desktop to a leg-and-rail assembly, bore a series of countersunk holes in each rail for the screws, before the legs are joined to the rail. Drill the holes on a drill press in two steps. First, bore holes at 6-inch intervals about halfway through the thickness of the rail. Clamp an edge guide to the drill press table to keep the holes in line. To accommodate the movement of the top, the holes should be larger than the diameter of the screw heads you will be using. In the second step, bore clearance holes slightly larger than the screw shank all the way through the rails *(right)*.

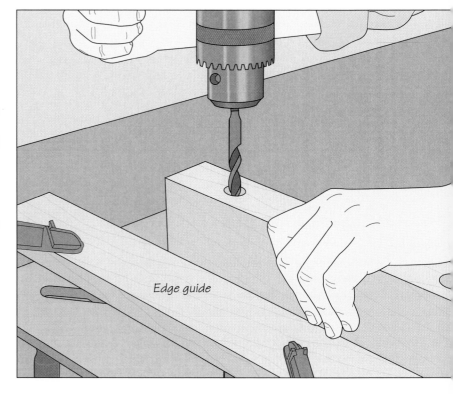

Edge guide

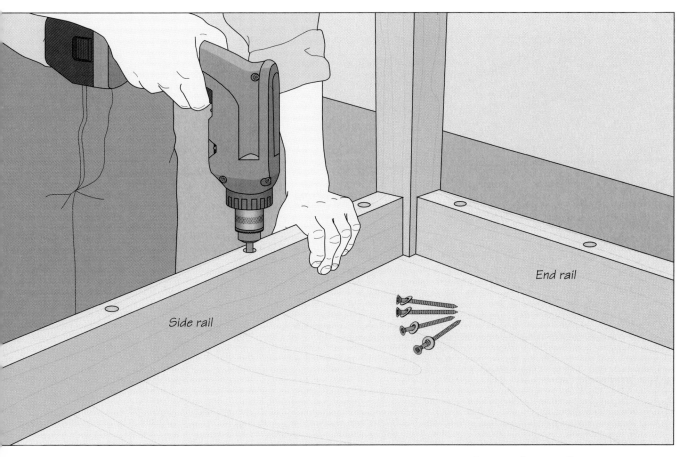

End rail

Side rail

SHOP TIP

Adding ledger strips

If you have a tabletop or desktop with thin rails that would be weakened by enlarged screw holes, you can screw ledger strips to the inside faces of the rails. Cut four strips to fit along the inside of the rails, and bore two sets of oversized holes in adjacent edges of each strip (page 96). Screw the ledger strips to all four rails, then attach the strips to the top.

2 Attaching the rails to the top
Set the top face-down on a work surface, and center the leg-and-rail assembly on it. Screw one side rail to the top first *(above)*, using washers to allow the wood to move. Square the top *(page 100)*, then screw the opposite side rail in place. Lastly, screw the two end rails to the top.

POCKET HOLES

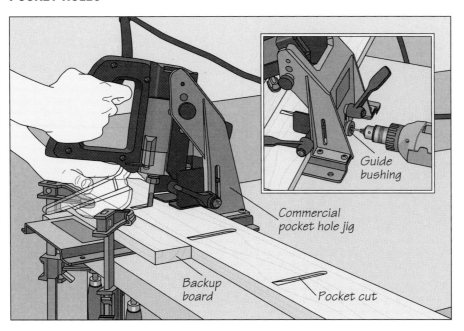

Commercial pocket hole jig

Guide bushing

Backup board

Pocket cut

Drilling the holes

You can use an electric drill and a commercial jig to drill pocket holes for attaching the top to a leg-and-rail assembly. Follow the manufacturer's instructions to adjust the jig to the desired depth of cut and clamp it to a work surface with a backup board against the stock. Plunge the bit into the wood, making the pocket cut *(left)*. Then, fit a drill with the bit supplied with the jig and bore a clearance hole connecting the pocket hole to the top of the rail, using the kit's guide bushing to direct the operation *(inset)*. Space pocket holes every 6 inches. Screw the top in place as shown on page 97.

WOOD BUTTONS

1 Making the buttons

To attach a top using wood buttons, you will need to place a wood button every 6 inches along the rails. Begin by cutting a groove on the inside face of each rail about ¾ inch from the top. You can cut several 1"-by-1¾" buttons from a single board; make the thickness of the stock equal to the gap between the bottom of the groove and the top of the rails, less ¹⁄₁₆ inch. Cut a rabbet to fit the groove at each end of the board, then rip the board into 1-inch strips on a band saw and cut off the buttons about 1¾ inches from the ends *(inset)*. To make holes in the buttons for installation, use an L-shaped corner jig fashioned from a scrap of ¾-inch plywood and two pieces of wood. Clamp the jig to your drill press table and steady the buttons with a hold-down fashioned from scrap wood. Bore through the centers on the unrabbeted portions of the buttons *(right)*.

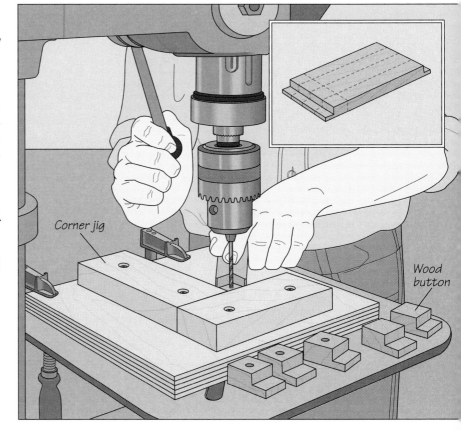

Corner jig

Wood button

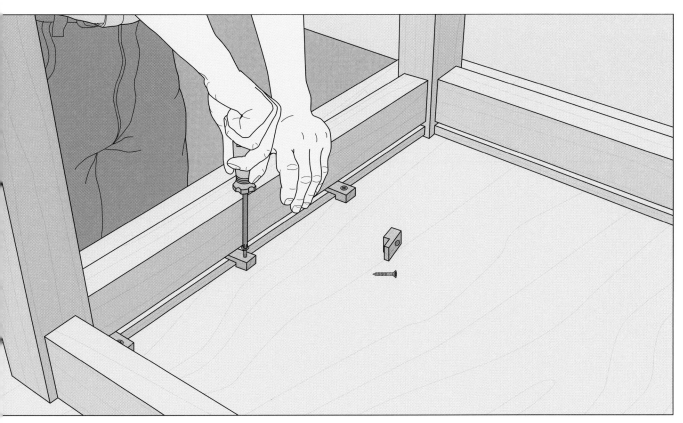

2 Installing the buttons
Center the glued-up leg-and-rail assembly on the tabletop and screw it to the top using the wood buttons you cut in step 1. Fit the rabbeted ends of the buttons into the groove in one of the side rails, spacing them every 6 inches. Screw the buttons in place *(above)*, leaving a ⅛-inch gap between the lipped ends of the buttons and the bottom of the groove to allow for wood movement. Square the top *(page 100)* and install the buttons at the opposite side. Lastly, install the buttons along the end rails.

SHOP TIP

Using steel tabletop fasteners
Commercial steel tabletop fasteners work like wood buttons: They are screwed to the tabletop from underneath and grip a groove routed or cut in the inside face of the rails. Because commercial fasteners are thinner than lipped wood buttons, the groove does not have to be cut with a dado blade; it can be made with a standard saw blade, or with a three-wing slotting cutter in a table-mounted router. To ensure proper tension, make the groove a little farther from the top than you would with the wood buttons.

DESKTOP FASTENERS

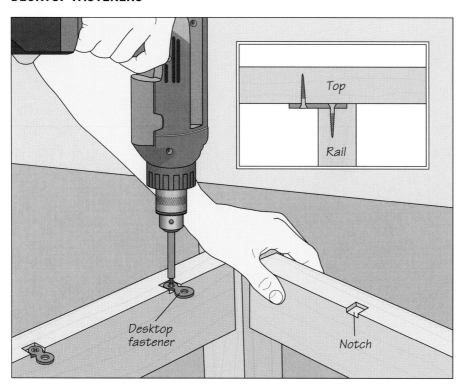

Desktop fastener

Notch

Top

Rail

Installing the fasteners

Desktop fasteners are a popular choice for attaching tops. Installed in shallow notches so they lie flush with the top of the rail they are then screwed into the top *(inset)*. The fasteners can pivot slightly back and forth as the top swells and shrinks. To install the fasteners, rout or chisel out recesses for them in the top of each rail, spacing the notches every 6 inches. Screw the hardware to the rails *(left)*, then center the leg-and-rail assembly on the top and screw it in place through the fasteners.

SQUARING THE TOP

Checking for square

Before screwing a top to a leg-and-rail assembly, make sure that the surface is centered and square. A bar clamp and wood pads will do this. Place the top good-side down on a work surface, set the leg-and-rail assembly on top, and attach one side rail to the top. Butt one jaw of a bar clamp against the edge of the top at one end, and the other jaw against a leg at the opposite end. Use wood pads to prevent marring the stock. Measure the distance between the edge of the top and the end rails at several points at both ends. All your measurements should be equal. If not, square the assembly by tightening the clamp *(right)*. Check the measurements, then screw the opposite side rail to the top. Remove the bar clamp and screw the end rails in place.

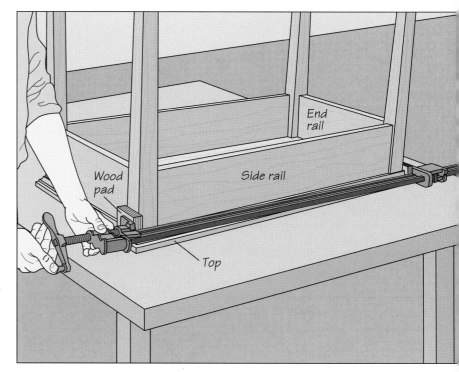

End rail

Side rail

Wood pad

Top

ADJUSTABLE TOPS

Not everyone has the space for a large dining table, although the extra surface area is often needed. One solution is a table with an expandable top. There are several choices open to you.

Drop-leaf tables typically have long leaves parallel with the grain that hang out of the way when not in use. Small leaves may be supported by a pull-out bar. Large leaves that more than double the surface area require swing legs or gate legs to be added.

Swing legs are part of a four-legged leg-and-rail assembly *(page 106)*; gate legs are an additional set of legs used specifically for support *(page 105)*. If you want to increase a table's length, exten-

Extension tables feature dividing tops that open in the middle to make room for spacer leaves. The mahogany dining table shown above slides open using commercial table extenders installed under both halves of the top. Steel tabletop eveners lock together when the top is closed, ensuring a flush surface.

sion tables feature tops that split open on sliders to accept additional spacer leaves. Extension tables can be built so that the entire table opens *(page 107)*, or just the top *(page 108)*.

Adjustable tops are made in much the same way as solid wood tops *(page 93)*, with a few important exceptions. Drop leaves are best glued up from quarter-sawn wood, where the growth rings are at right angles to the face. This will reduce the tendency of the wood to cup. Since it shrinks and swells less than plain-sawn stock, quartersawn wood is also ideal for the tops of extension tables, where the grain runs across the width of the table.

MAKING A RULE JOINT FOR A DROP-LEAF TABLE

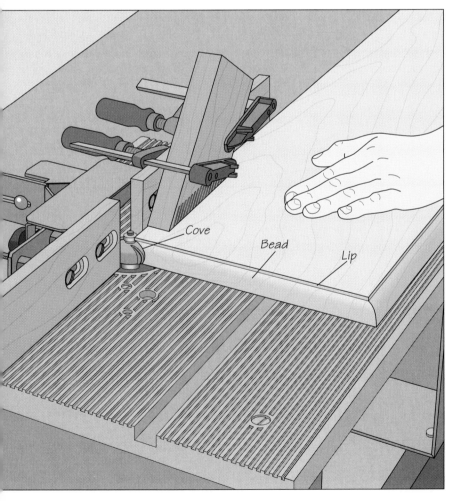

Cove

Bead

Lip

1 Routing the cove in the leaves
The easiest way to make a rule joint is by using a matched set of piloted cove and round-over router bits. First, install the round-over bit in your router and shape a bead around the tabletop and the three outside edges of the leaves. Make the cut in several passes, leaving a ⅛-inch lip around the edge. Then install the piloted cove bit and mount the router in a table. Align the fence with the bit pilot so the width of cut equals one-half the cutter diameter. Set the depth of cut shallow at first; make several passes to reach your final depth gradually. Feed the table leaf into the bit, pressing the edge of the workpiece firmly against the fence *(left)*. After each pass, test-fit the pieces until the tabletop and the leaf mesh with a very slight gap between the two.

Shorter hinge leaf

Longer hinge leaf

2 Installing the rule joint hinge

Position the shorter hinge leaf against the underside of the tabletop and the longer hinge leaf against the table leaf; the hinge pin should be aligned with the start of the round-over cut on the tabletop *(inset)*. Offset the hinge pin ½₂ inch toward the edge of the tabletop for clearance. Outline the hinge on both the tabletop and the leaf and rout out the waste. Chisel out the mortises to accept the hinge pins *(above)*, then screw the hinges in place.

SUPPORTING A DROP LEAF

Using a commercial drop-leaf support

Cut a notch in the middle of the rail adjacent to the table leaf to accommodate the support. (For drop leaves more than 3 feet long, use two supports, located about 6 inches from each end.) With the leaves installed and the tabletop attached, set the table upside-down on a work surface. Slide the support in the notch, positioning it so that it fully supports the leaf, and screw it in place *(right)*.

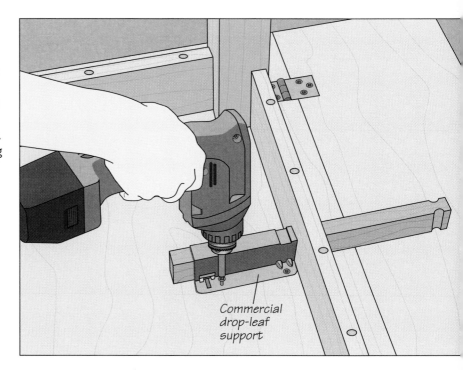

Commercial drop-leaf support

DROP-LEAF SUPPORTS

If commercial drop-leaf supports are too bulky for your table, you can easily make supports that will complement your design. Before attaching the leg-and-rail assembly to the tabletop, cut two notches in the top edge of each side rail adjoining a drop leaf. The notches should be about 6 inches from the ends of the rail and sized to fit the supports you will make. For each leaf, cut two supports from the same stock you used to build your table. The supports should be sufficient to hold the drop leaf; the one in the illustrations at right is cut 2 inches wide and 14 inches long from ¾-inch-thick stock.

To prepare the supports, you need to rout two grooves down the middle of each one to accommodate screws and washers. Cut one groove halfway through the support slightly wider than the washers you will use *(inset)*; center the second groove in the first one, making it slightly wider than the screw shanks and cutting right through the support. Both grooves should stop 2 inches from each end of the support.

Attach a knob to one end of the support to make it easy to slide in the rail notch. Set the fully assembled table upside down on a work surface, slide the support into the notch, and position it so that it supports the leaf. Install a screw and washer into the top at the inside end of the groove, driving the screw until it meets the washer *(right, top)*. This screw will be the support's outward stop. To mount the inward stop, retract the slide so the knob-end is flush with the rail, and install a second screw and washer the same way as the first *(right, bottom)*.

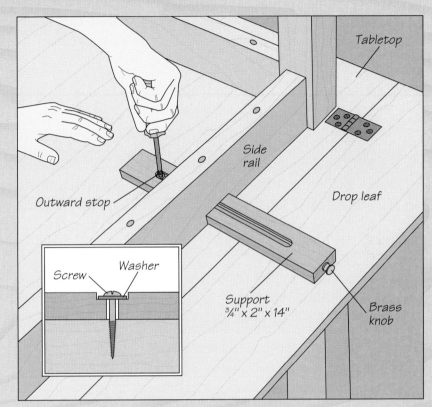

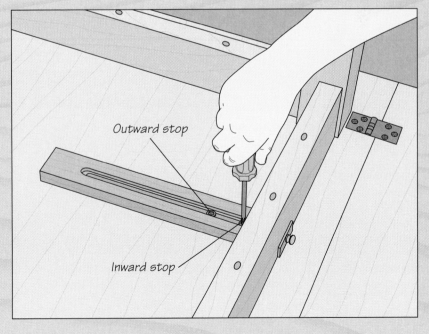

PIVOTING DROP-LEAF SUPPORTS

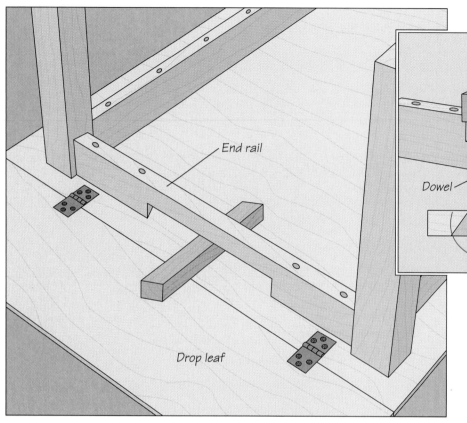

Pivoting drop-leaf support

Dowel

End rail

Drop leaf

SHOP TIP

Leveling drop leaves
Drop leaves that droop
can be leveled easily
with a shallow
wedge. Glue
the piece of
wood to the
underside of
the leaf in line with
the drop-leaf support.
The wedge will jack
the leaf up when the
support is slid
into position.

Making and installing the pivot rail
An alternate method of buttressing drop
leaves is with pivoting supports. Housed
in a notched section of the table rail, the
support pivots on a dowel to hold the
drop leaf when the leaf is extended
(above, left), then aligns with the rail
when the leaf is not needed. Begin by
cutting the supports from the same stock
used for the table: Make one for a drop
leaf that adjoins an end rail, and two for
a leaf adjacent to a side rail. The supports should be as thick as the rails, one-
half their width, and twice as long as the
distance between the rail and the middle
of the drop leaf when the table is assembled. Angle the ends of the support and
notch the top edge of the rail to match.
This will allow the support to close almost
flush with the rail. Bore a hole in the
centers of the support and the notch for
a dowel or a blind pivot hinge; each
hole should be slightly deeper than one-
half the dowel or hinge length. Glue the
dowel or install the hinge in the hole in
the rail *(inset)*, place the support on the
dowel, and assemble the table.

GATE LEGS FOR A SIX-LEGGED TABLE

1 Installing the gate legs
On six-legged gateleg tables, the table leaves are supported by two swinging gate legs hinged to the table rails and stretchers. The table shown at right has a standard four-legged leg-and-rail assembly, an additional set of rails, called stretchers, installed near the bottom of the legs, and two gate legs. The tabletop is connected to two leaves with rule joints *(pages 101-102)*. The central portion of the top can be narrower than on a drop-leaf table, but the width of the leaves should not exceed the height of the table, or the leaves will touch the floor when they are not in use. The gate legs are attached after the base is joined to the tabletop *(pages 96-99)*. Cut four gateleg rails: two to join the gate legs to the table rails, and two more to connect the legs to the stretchers. The rails should be long enough to hold the gate legs near the center of the leaves. Join the gate rails to the legs with mortise-and-tenon joints *(page 76)*; use hinges to fasten the rails near the middle of the stretchers and table rails *(right)*, making sure the gate legs will rest between the fixed legs when the leaves are down.

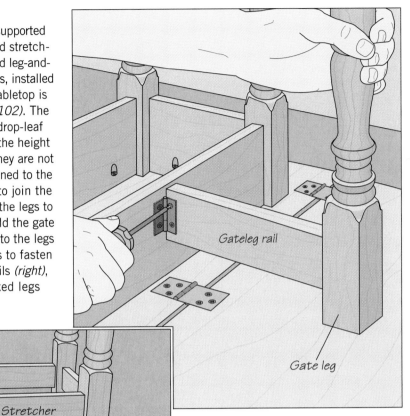

Gateleg rail

Gate leg

Stretcher

Gateleg stop

2 Installing gateleg stops
Use wooden stops to hold the gate legs in place when the leaves are in use. Set the table upside down on a work surface and swing open the gate legs until they are centered on the leaves. Butt a small wood block against the outside of each gate leg and screw it to the underside of the leaf *(left)*.

Swing legs were traditionally attached to table rails with wooden hinges. Sometimes called knuckle joints, these were made by cutting interlocking fingers into the hinge rail and the swing-leg rail. The two rails were then connected by a wooden or metal pin. These joints are still used on reproductions of antique swing-leg tables. On most modern tables, a metal cranked hinge is now used.

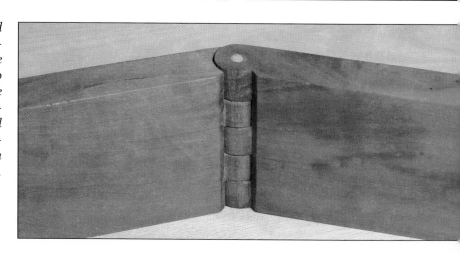

SWING LEGS FOR A FOUR-LEGGED TABLE

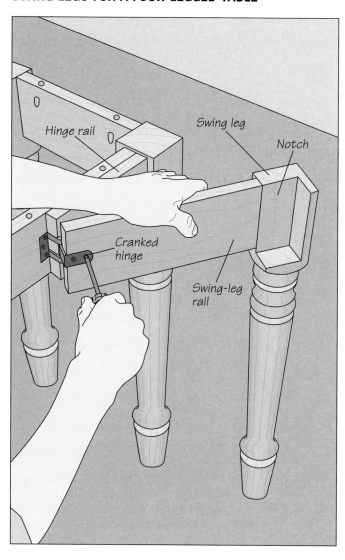

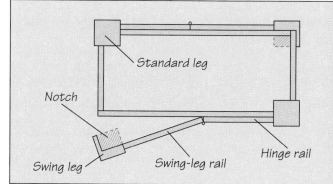

Using a cranked hinge

In a four-legged swing-leg table, there are two fixed legs and two swing legs that pivot out to support the leaves *(above)*. To assemble this table, first prepare a top with a rule joint *(pages 101-102)*, then make four legs and rails, making any necessary preparations for the method you will use later to attach the top *(page 96-99)*. Join only two legs to the rails at opposite corners; use mortise-and-tenon joints *(page 76)*. Set the two other legs aside as swing legs, and join the rails at the two remaining corners with dovetail or box joints. Next, cut the hinge and swing-leg rails, one for each swing leg. Cut recesses in the table rails, the swing-leg rails, and the hinge rails for the cranked hinge; this will allow the swing-leg rails to sit flush against the table rails. Also cut a notch in the legs so they will wrap around the table rails when the leaves are down. Screw the hinge rails to the table rails and join the swing-leg rails to the swing legs with mortise-and-tenon joints. Fasten the swing legs in place with cranked hinges, screwing one leaf of the hinge to the table rail and the other to the swing-leg rail *(left)*. Now place the tabletop top-side down, position the swing-leg assembly in place, and screw the two together.

DIVIDING EXTENSION TABLES

1 Positioning the table extenders

To make a dividing extension table with legs and rails that move when the top is expanded, build a leg-and-rail assembly and a top. But rather than attaching them, cut both in half on your table saw. (To ensure that the tabletop halves do not expand at different rates as a result of humidity changes, align the grain of the top across its width.) Attach the leg-and-rail assemblies to the top halves, making sure the cut edges of the rails and tops align perfectly. The commercial table extenders shown on this page are screwed to the underside of the tabletop halves. To determine the position of the extenders, set the table halves upside down on a work surface and mark lines on the underside of the tops 4 to 6 inches from the side rails. To ensure the lines are perpendicular to the joint between the top halves, use a carpenter's square *(right)*.

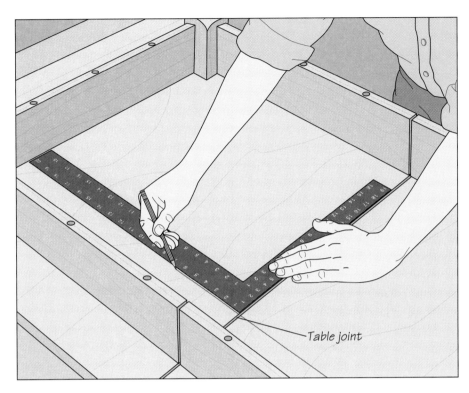

Table joint

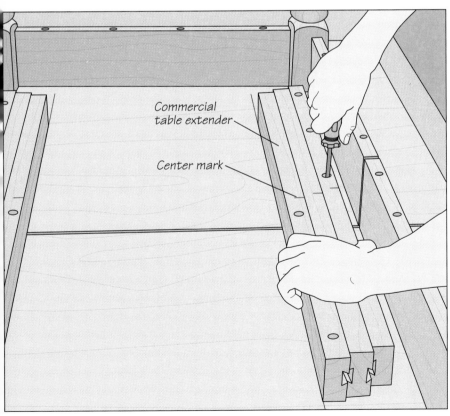

Commercial table extender

Center mark

2 Installing the table extenders

Mark the center of each segment of the table extenders with a pencil. Then position the extenders face down on the underside of the tabletop, aligning the center marks with the joint between table halves and the inside segments with the lines you marked in step 1. Before screwing the extenders down, open them slightly; this ensures that there will be no gap between the top halves when the table is closed. With the tabletop halves butted together and ends flush, screw the outside segments of the extenders to the top, driving screws through the predrilled holes *(left)*. Cut a leaf to fit the opening between the top halves.

NON-DIVIDING EXTENSION TABLES

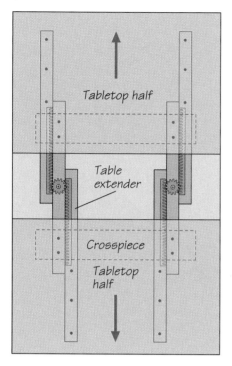

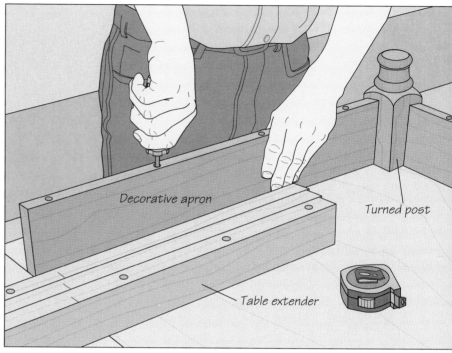

Decorative apron

Turned post

Table extender

1 Making the decorative apron

On a non-dividing extension table—with tabletop halves that open while the leg-and-rail assembly remains stationary—the top halves are attached to the outside movable segments of the extenders and the rails are fastened to crosspieces that are screwed to the middle fixed extender segments *(above, left)*. Start by cutting the top in half. Now build a decorative apron-and-post assembly for each tabletop half and screw each in place *(above, right)*. The aprons and posts are joined *(page 76)* and attached to the top *(page 96)* in the same fashion as a leg-and-rail assembly. Fasten the table extenders to the top halves as you would for a dividing extension table *(page 107)*. At this point, the assembly is like an ordinary dividing table, with corner posts in place of legs.

2 Preparing the leg-and-rail assembly

To support the table, you must now build a leg-and-rail assembly that will fit inside the decorative apron. To attach the crosspieces that join the assembly to the table extenders, cut four notches in the top edge of the side rails using a chisel and a wooden mallet *(right)*. Make sure the notches in opposite rails are perfectly aligned. Screw the crosspieces to the rails.

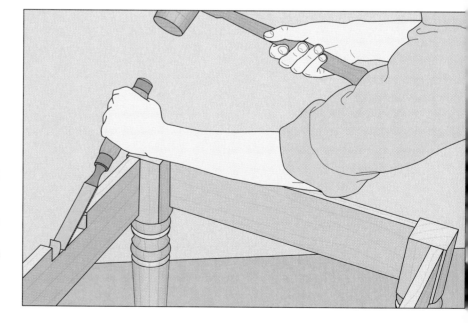

3 Attaching the leg-and-rail assembly to the table extenders

Complete the table with the top upside down on a work surface. Center the leg-and-rail assembly inside the decorative apron. The crosspieces will rest on the fixed segments of the table extenders. Screw them in place *(right)*. Cut a leaf to fit the opening in the table.

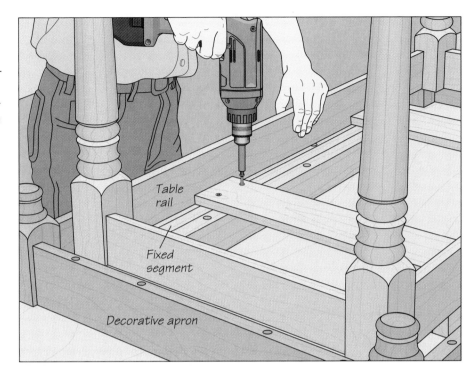

Table rail

Fixed segment

Decorative apron

PEDESTAL EXTENSION TABLES

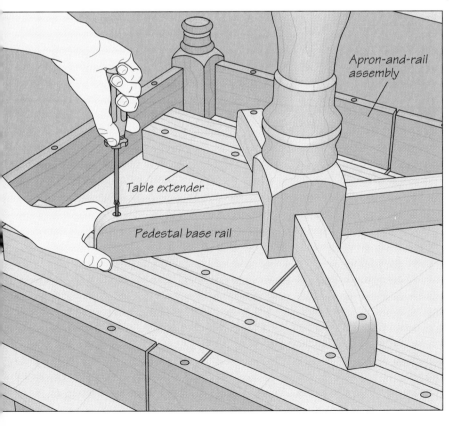

Apron-and-rail assembly

Table extender

Pedestal base rail

Attaching the base to the top

To make an extension table with a pedestal base, start with a top and an apron-and-post assembly like that of a non-dividing extension table *(page 108)*. Attach the outside sliding segments of two table extenders to the top halves. You are now ready to attach the base to the fixed portion of the extenders. Make sure the rails of the pedestal base extend beyond the fixed segments, and bore holes for countersinking screws through the rails. Align the holes over the middle fixed segments of the extenders and screw them together.

INSTALLING LEAVES ON A TRESTLE TABLE

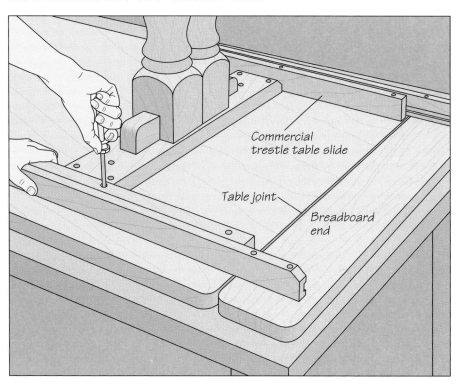

Commercial trestle table slide

Table joint

Breadboard end

1 Installing trestle table slides
To install spacer leaves on a trestle table, first cut and rout two "breadboard" ends using the same bit you used to shape the rest of the tabletop. Then set the table upside down on a work surface, align the breadboard ends with the end of the top, and position two commercial trestle table slides face-down on the top's underside. The ends of the slides' inside segments should be flush with the joint between the table and the breadboard ends; the slides should also be parallel to the tabletop edges. Screw the inside segments of the slides to the tabletop *(left)*. Before screwing the outside segments to the breadboard ends, open the slides slightly to ensure that there will be no gaps in the top when the table is closed.

2 Installing the spacer leaves
Cut and shape spacer leaves to fit between the top and the breadboard ends. Make the leaves slightly narrower than the table opening so they can be inserted and removed easily. To hold each leaf in alignment when installed, use dowels at its breadboard-end edge and tabletop eveners *(page 92)* at the other edge. For the dowels, bore holes in the edge of the breadboard end and the leaf *(page 74)*, then glue the dowels in the leaf. Screw three pairs of eveners to the underside of the leaf at the other edge and the tabletop. To use the spacer leaves, extend each breadboard end fully, set the leaf in place *(right)*, and push the table closed until the dowels fit into their holes and all the pieces butt together.

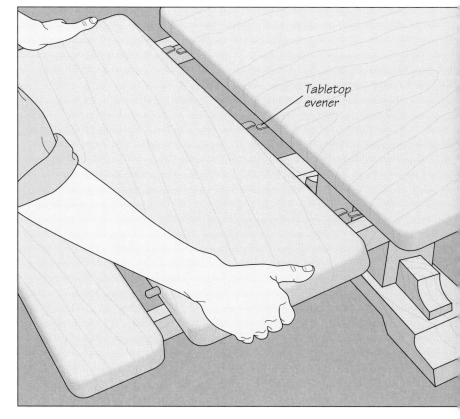

Tabletop evener

TABLE-LOCKING HARDWARE

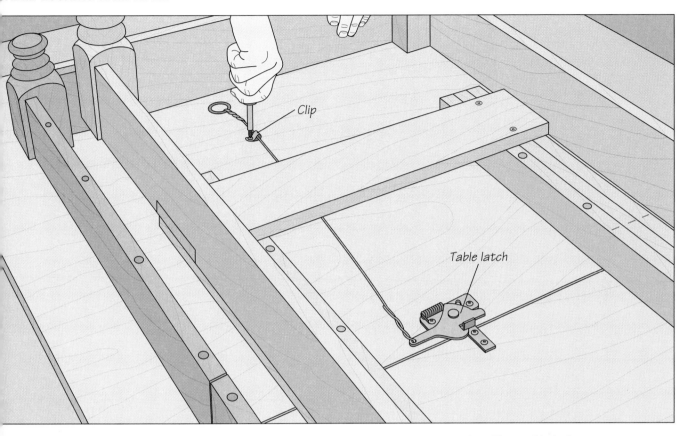

Clip

Table latch

Installing a table lock

To prevent an extension table from sliding open when it is moved, install table-locking hardware on the underside of the top. The table lock shown normally keeps the top halves together. By simply reaching under the end of the table and pulling on the wire, the latch is opened. To install the table lock, center and screw the latch on the table joint. Then extend the wire to one end and fix it in place using the screw and clip provided (above).

SHOP TIP

Aligning table leaves with dowel centers

To keep table leaves properly aligned with table-tops, mating holes for dowels or alignment pins must line up precisely. Dowel centers are ideal for this task. For the table shown here, bore holes in one edge of the leaf and insert dowel centers. Then align the leaf with the top and butt them together, making sure their ends are aligned. The pointed ends of the dowel centers will punch impressions on the edge of the top, providing starting points for boring the mating holes.

DECORATIVE ELEMENTS

A glass top can lighten the look of a large table. The top can either consist of a single pane of glass, or incorporate glass as a design element, as in the framed-glass top of the mahogany coffee table shown at right.

INSTALLING A FRAMED-GLASS TOP

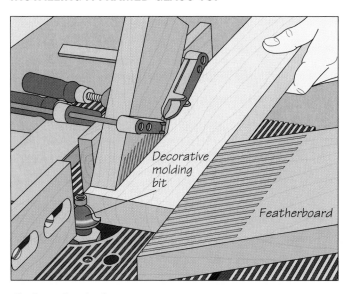

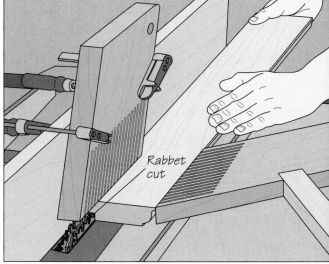

1 Preparing the frame
Prepare the four frame pieces by shaping their outside edges and rabbeting the inside edges to hold the glass. Use stock that is at least ¾ inch thick and 2½ inches wide. For the shaping cuts, install a decorative molding bit in your router and mount the tool in a table. Use three featherboards to support the workpiece: two clamped to the fence on either side of the bit and one secured to the table. Feed the stock face-down *(above,*

left). To cut the rabbets, attach an auxiliary wooden fence to your table saw and install a dado head, adjusting its width to the rabbet width—about ½ inch. Set the cutting height to the glass thickness. Using three featherboards to support the workpiece, position the fence for the width of cut and saw the rabbets *(above, right).* (In both illustrations, the featherboard on the outfeed side of the fence has been removed for clarity.)

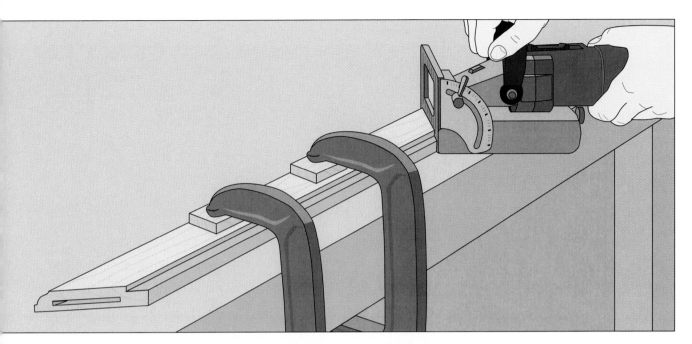

2 Gluing up the frame and installing the glass

Once you have shaped and rabbeted the frame pieces, cut them to length with 45° miters at their ends. For added strength, join the corners with biscuit joints. Clamp the pieces to a work surface and use a plate joiner to cut mating slots in the mitered ends *(above)*. Insert glue and one biscuit at each corner *(left)* and clamp the frame together. Next, attach the frame to the leg-and-rail assembly of your table *(page 96)*. Measure the opening in the frame and have a sheet of tempered glass at least ¼-inch thick cut to fit. To install the glass, glue strips of felt into the rabbets to act as a cushion *(inset)*, then set the glass in the frame.

Biscuit

Frame

Glass

Felt

INSTALLING A LEATHER TOP

1 Gluing leather to a base panel
Tops for tables and desks can incorporate leather in their design. This example features a leather-covered panel surrounded by a wood frame. To start, cut a piece of leather to cover the face and edges of a base panel, typically ¾-inch plywood; using leather that weighs at least 4 ounces per square foot (about 1/16 inch thick) will prevent the surface of the panel from showing through the leather. Use contact cement to attach the material to the face of the panel and smooth it down *(right)*. To enable the leather to bond cleanly around the edges, cut out small squares at each corner *(inset)*. Then glue it to the edges.

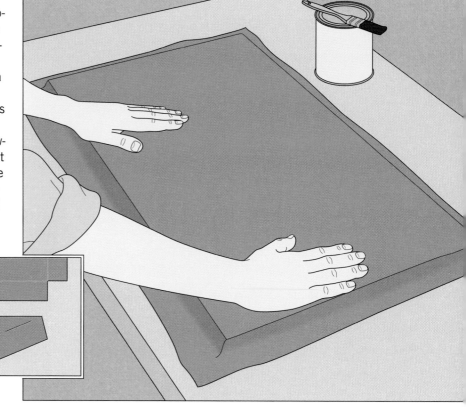

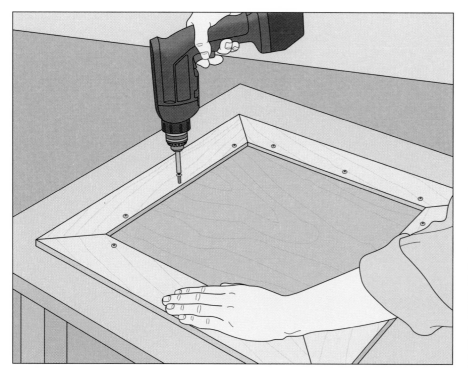

2 Installing the panel in a frame
Make and glue up a tabletop frame for the leathered panel as you would for a glass-framed top *(page 112)*. Fit the panel in the frame and set the assembly upside down on a work surface. Fasten the panel to the frame, spacing screws at 6- to 8-inch intervals *(left)*.

INSTALLING A TILE TOP

Ceramic, marble, or slate tiles can also be incorporated into tops for tables or desks. Making a tile top is much like making a leather one (page 114). The tiles are glued to a substrate of ¾-inch plywood, which is then screwed to a tabletop frame. As the tiles are being glued down, rubber spacers are installed to maintain the proper spacing. Once the adhesive dries, the spacers are removed and the gaps between the tiles are grouted.

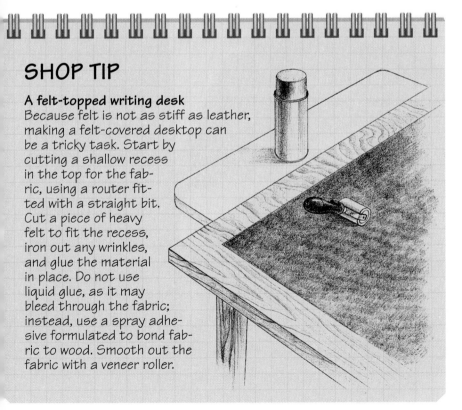

SHOP TIP

A felt-topped writing desk
Because felt is not as stiff as leather, making a felt-covered desktop can be a tricky task. Start by cutting a shallow recess in the top for the fabric, using a router fitted with a straight bit. Cut a piece of heavy felt to fit the recess, iron out any wrinkles, and glue the material in place. Do not use liquid glue, as it may bleed through the fabric; instead, use a spray adhesive formulated to bond fabric to wood. Smooth out the fabric with a veneer roller.

DRAWERS

Rather than measuring a drawer opening with a tape or a rule, use the drawer parts themselves. Here, a drawer side is inserted into its opening and a cutting line is marked on the stock in line with the front edge of the opening. A shim at the back will ensure that the drawer is slightly shorter than the opening and will not close against the back of the carcase.

Virtually all desks and many tables need drawers. And no matter what their use, all drawers must meet essentially the same requirements. Whether you are making three or four sturdy drawers for a desk pedestal, like the one shown in the photo on page 116, or a single unit for an end table, each drawer must fit precisely and withstand considerable stress, while also complementing the design of the furniture that holds it.

The first step in building a drawer is to consider its use. What will the drawer contain? How much use will it receive? These matters will determine the type of wood and joinery you choose.

Start with the drawer front. It is not only the most visible piece, it also undergoes the most stress. A solid, durable joint is required to keep it firmly attached to the sides. Joinery methods are shown beginning on page 120. The front should also blend attractively with the grain of the wood surrounding it. For structural reasons, the grain of the front should run horizontally. Vertical grain will not produce solid joints; it will also be prone to greater movement with moisture changes.

The stock you use for the drawer sides and back does not have to be the same as for the front—provided you choose a durable wood that is resistant to warping. Ash, oak, maple, and cherry are all strong enough to withstand heavy use. Softer species like pine and poplar are usable, but only for smaller drawers. Some cabinetmakers choose contrasting woods like walnut and ash for the front and sides to highlight the joinery when the drawer is opened.

Beyond appearance and strength, a drawer must fit perfectly. A drawer that jams or chatters when it is opened and closed will wear more quickly than one that whispers quietly. There are several ways to mount drawers, as shown beginning on page 133. Each method is designed to support the drawer, prevent it from tipping as it is pulled out, and stop it as it slides home. Preparing dust frames for bottom-run drawers is shown in the Casework chapter *(page 28)*. The section on drawer stops *(page 138)* presents several effective ways to stop drawers from being pulled out or pushed in too far.

Hardware adds the final touch to a drawer. The selection shown on page 119 offers some suggestions. Locks are applied to drawers both for securing valuables and to copy traditional pieces. Steps for installing a half-mortise lock are shown starting on page 131.

Combining strength with appearance, half-blind dovetails are a popular choice for joining drawer fronts to sides. Here, a dovetailed drawer is slid into one side of a double-pedestal desk.

ANATOMY OF A DRAWER

A drawer is essentially an open box, consisting of a front, a back, two sides, and a bottom. The front is most often made from thicker stock than the sides and back; the bottom is typically made from ¼-inch plywood. Beyond these general similarities, drawers vary in style, methods of joinery, and techniques of mounting. Many drawer-making options are illustrated below and on the following page.

Three popular drawer front styles are shown directly below. Installing a drawer can be a tricky operation, especially if the drawer is poorly made. An out-of-square drawer can sometimes be concealed with a false front, but if it is badly twisted, it will be almost impossible to install so that it opens smoothly. Several joints for assembling drawers are also shown below; each possesses different qualities of strength and durability.

Installing hardware is the final, and usually the simplest, step in building a drawer. The selection of drawer hardware shown on page 119 will provide you with many options.

Flush front: *Allows the drawer to fit entirely within the carcase; also known as an inset drawer*

Lipped front: *A rabbeted front creates a lip that is useful for concealing commercial runners when the drawer is closed. Lip performs double duty as drawer stop*

False front: *A separate front is attached to the structural front; conceals end grain of drawer sides*

DRAWER JOINTS

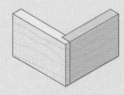

Rabbet
For back-to-side joints; also strong enough for joining the front to the sides if reinforced with screws or nails. Suitable for solid wood or plywood

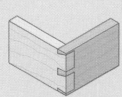

Through dovetail
Strong, decorative joint for any drawer corner; end grain of drawer sides can be concealed with false front. Appropriate for solid wood but not plywood

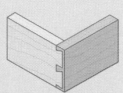

Half-blind dovetail
The traditional joint for connecting the front to the sides; conceals end grain of sides. Suitable only for solid wood

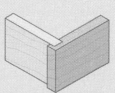

Dado
Commonly to join the back to the sides; for solid wood or plywood

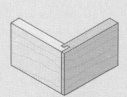

Double dado
For any corner of a drawer; conceals end grain of sides. Suitable only for solid wood

DRAWER HARDWARE

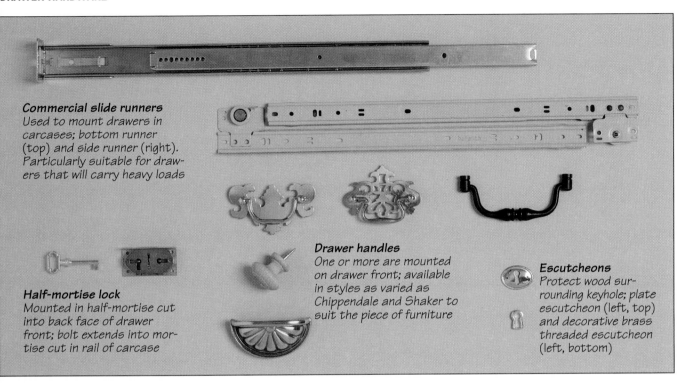

Commercial slide runners
Used to mount drawers in carcases; bottom runner (top) and side runner (right). Particularly suitable for drawers that will carry heavy loads

Half-mortise lock
Mounted in half-mortise cut into back face of drawer front; bolt extends into mortise cut in rail of carcase

Drawer handles
One or more are mounted on drawer front; available in styles as varied as Chippendale and Shaker to suit the piece of furniture

Escutcheons
Protect wood surrounding keyhole; plate escutcheon (left, top) and decorative brass threaded escutcheon (left, bottom)

DRAWER-MOUNTING METHODS

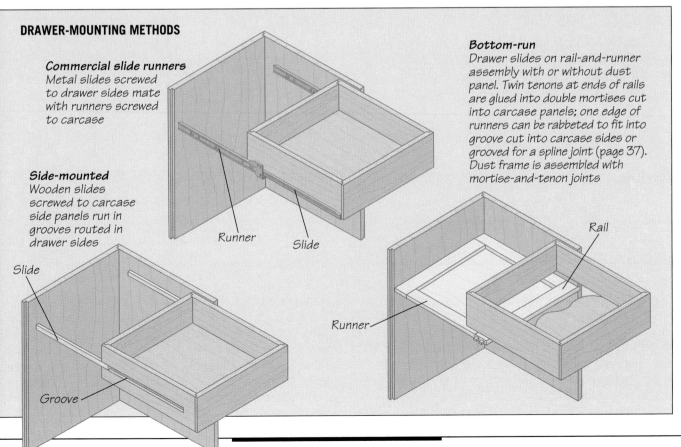

Commercial slide runners
Metal slides screwed to drawer sides mate with runners screwed to carcase

Side-mounted
Wooden slides screwed to carcase side panels run in grooves routed in drawer sides

Bottom-run
Drawer slides on rail-and-runner assembly with or without dust panel. Twin tenons at ends of rails are glued into double mortises cut into carcase panels; one edge of runners can be rabbeted to fit into groove cut into carcase sides or grooved for a spline joint (page 37). Dust frame is assembled with mortise-and-tenon joints

Runner

Slide

Slide

Groove

Rail

Runner

DRAWER JOINERY

When you have settled on the size of a drawer, it is time to choose the right joinery. Since the corners of a drawer undergo different stresses, choose your joints accordingly. The front-to-side connections endure the most stress and require the strongest joinery. The connections between the back and sides are less affected by everyday use and therefore do not have to be as solid.

The following pages present several joinery options. Three of them—the half-blind (below) and through dovetail (page 125), and the double dado (page 127)—can only be used with solid wood. Each of these joints is strong enough to connect the front to the sides, although the double dado should be reserved for small, light-duty drawers. For plywood drawers, use a rabbet joint for any of the connections, or a standard dado joint to attach the back piece to the sides.

Different joints for different needs: A dado-and-rabbet joint works well for attaching the back to the sides of a drawer. The front demands a stronger joint that will conceal the end grain of the sides—in this case, a double dado.

The joinery options you choose will also affect the appearance of the drawer. Unless you are installing a false front, choose a joint like the half-blind dovetail or double dado to conceal the end grain of the sides.

Drawer bottoms fit into a groove cut in the sides and front. The groove can be cut with a saw before the joinery cuts are made (page 123) or once the drawer is assembled, using a table-mounted router and a three-wing slotting cutter.

Before gluing up, make sure you have decided on a mounting method. A side-hung drawer, for example, needs to have a groove cut in its side before the drawer is assembled (page 133).

Before you begin cutting, select the most attractive face of each part and mark it with an X to designate it as the outside of the drawer. Reserve the most visually appealing piece for the front.

HALF-BLIND DOVETAIL JOINTS

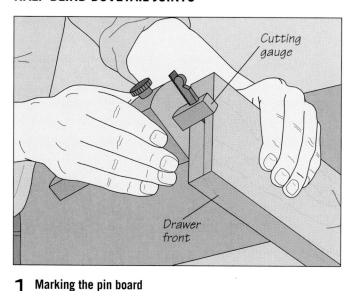

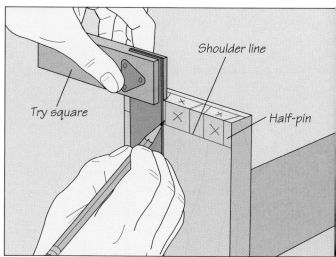

1 Marking the pin board

Mark the outside faces of all the boards with an X. Then set a cutting gauge to about two-thirds the thickness of the pin board—the drawer front—and mark a line across the end, closer to the outside than the inside face *(above, left)*. Adjust the cutting gauge to the thickness of the drawer sides and scribe a line on the inside face of the front to mark the shoulder line of the tails. Next, use a dovetail square to outline the pins on an end of the front; the wide part of the pins should be on the

inside face of the stock so the front does not pull away from the sides. There are no strict guidelines for spacing dovetail pins, but for most drawers, a half-pin at each edge and two evenly spaced pins in between makes a strong and attractive joint. To complete the marking, secure the front in a vise and use a try square and a pencil to extend the lines on the board end to the shoulder line on its inside face *(above, right)*. Mark the waste sections with Xs as you go.

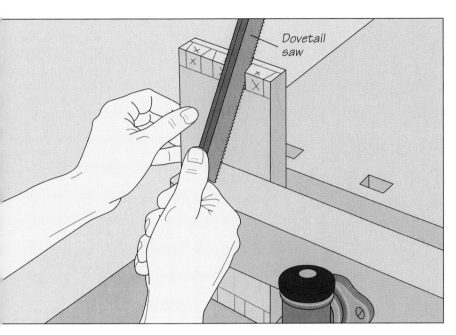

Dovetail saw

2 Cutting the pins

Secure the drawer front in a vise with the inside face of the stock toward you, then cut along the edges of the pins with a dovetail saw *(left)*, working your way from one board edge to the other. (Some woodworkers prefer to cut all the left-hand edges of the pins, then move on to the right-hand edges.) Hold the board steady and align the saw blade just to the waste side of the cutting line; angle the saw toward the waste to avoid cutting into the pins. Use smooth, even strokes, allowing the saw to cut on the push stroke. Continue the cut to the shoulder line, then repeat to saw the pins at the other end of the board.

3 Chiseling out the waste

Lay the drawer front inside-face up on a work surface and clamp a guide block to it, aligning its edge with the waste side of the shoulder line. Starting at one edge of the stock, hold the flat side of a chisel against the guide block; the blade should be no wider than the narrowest portion of the waste section. With the chisel perpendicular to the board face, strike the handle with a wooden mallet, making a ⅛-inch-deep cut into the waste *(right)*. Then hold the chisel bevel-up about ⅛ inch below the board face and peel away a thin layer of waste. Continue until you reach the scribed line on the end of the board. Repeat the process with the remaining waste sections, then pare away any excess waste *(step 4)*.

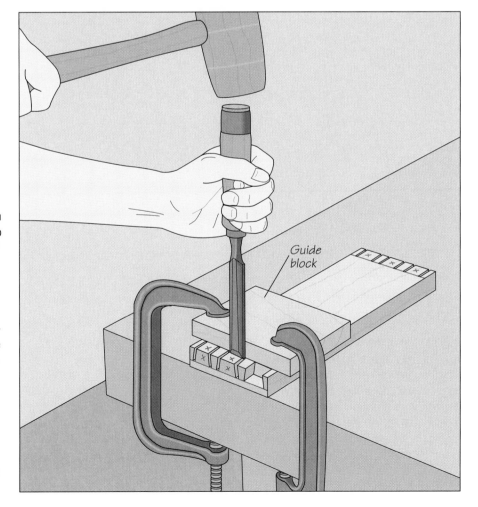

Guide block

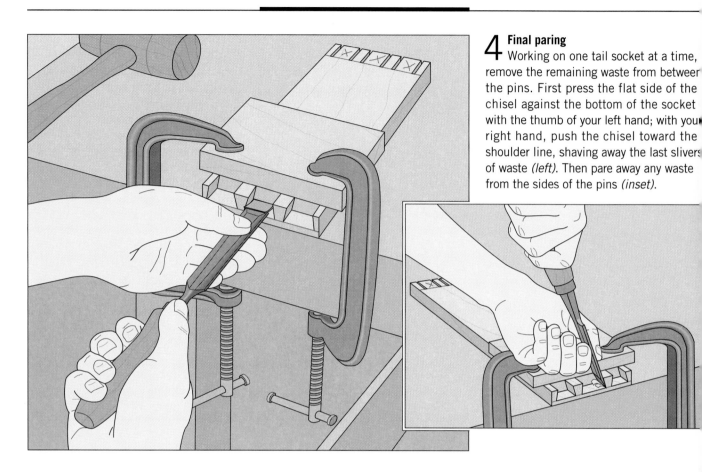

4 Final paring
Working on one tail socket at a time, remove the remaining waste from between the pins. First press the flat side of the chisel against the bottom of the socket with the thumb of your left hand; with your right hand, push the chisel toward the shoulder line, shaving away the last slivers of waste *(left)*. Then pare away any waste from the sides of the pins *(inset)*.

5 Laying out the tails
Set one drawer side outside-face down on the work surface. Hold the drawer front end-down with its inside face aligned with the shoulder line of the tail board, making certain the edges of the boards are flush. Outline the tails with a pencil *(right)*, then use a try square to extend the lines on the end of the board. Mark all the waste sections with Xs.

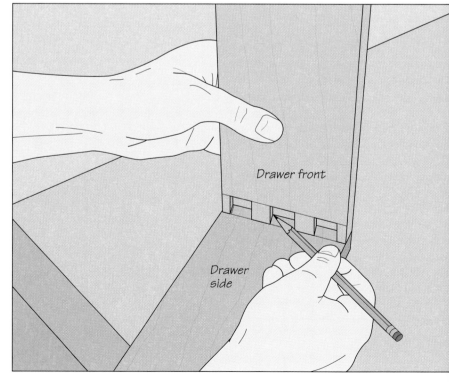

Drawer front

Drawer side

6 Cutting the tails

Use a dovetail saw to cut the tails the same way you cut the pins *(step 2)*. Angling the board *(right)*, rather than the saw, makes for easier cutting. Secure the board so that the right-hand edges of the tails are vertical. Saw smoothly and evenly along the edges of the tails, stopping at the shoulder line. Reposition the board in the vise to cut the left-hand edges. Once all the saw cuts have been made, remove the waste with a chisel as in steps 3 and 4. To avoid splitting the tails, remove about half the waste, then flip the workpiece over to chisel out the remaining waste.

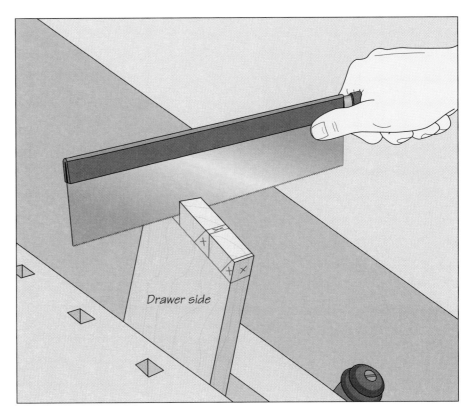

Drawer side

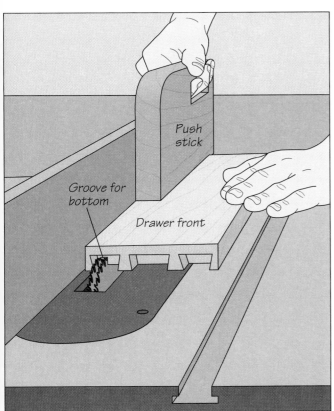

Push stick

Groove for bottom

Drawer front

7 Preparing the drawer for a bottom panel

Dry-fit the drawer and mark any spots where the joints bind; use a chisel to pare small amounts of wood to achieve a good fit. Loose joints can be tightened *(page 124)*. Next, use your table saw to cut a groove in the drawer front and sides to accommodate the bottom. Install a dado head, adjusting its width to the thickness of the stock you plan to use for the bottom (typically ¼ inch). Mark the groove on the drawer front and sides; the groove should be located just above the half-pin at the bottom edge of the front. Align the groove mark with the dado head and position the rip fence against the edge of the stock. Adjust the blade height for the depth of the groove (no more than one-half the stock thickness). Feed the drawer front across the table using a push stick *(left)*. **(Caution: Blade guard removed for clarity.)** Repeat the cut on the drawer sides. Then install a combination blade and trim the bottom of the back flush with the top of the grooves in the sides and front. This will allow the bottom to slide into position when the drawer is assembled.

Clamping block

8 Gluing up the drawer

Before assembling the drawer, cut a bottom panel from ¼-inch plywood or solid stock to fit the drawer opening, adding the depth of the grooves (less ¹⁄₁₆ inch) to its width and the depth of one groove and the thickness of the back panel to its length. To glue up dovetail joints, clamping pressure should be applied to the tail boards. (On the drawer shown above, the back is joined to the sides with through dovetails.) To distribute clamping pressure properly, make a specially notched clamping block for each joint. Each block should be as long as the width of the stock and notched so it only touches the tails and does not exert pressure on the pins. Spread glue evenly on all the contacting surfaces of the boards and assemble the joints. Install a bar clamp along each pin board, then tighten the clamps a little at a time *(above)*. Check the drawer for square *(page 128)* and adjust the clamping pressure, if necessary.

SHOP TIP

Fixing dovetails

Even experienced woodworkers cut the occasional dovetail that fits a little loosely. In most cases, small gaps can be filled to improve the fit and appearance of the joint. Cut small wooden wedges from the same wood as the drawer, tapering them so they will slide into the openings. Spread glue on the wedges and use a wooden mallet to tap them in place. Sand any protrusions flush with the surface of the drawer.

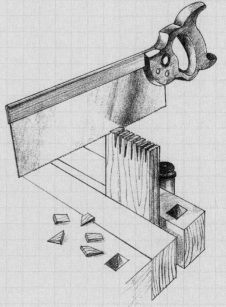

THROUGH DOVETAILS

1 Marking the pin board

The through dovetail is similar to the half-blind joint, except that the tails extend fully through the pin board. To begin marking the joints, make an X on the outside faces of all the boards. Then set a cutting gauge to the thickness of the stock and scribe a line along both ends of the boards to mark the shoulder of the pins and tails. Next secure the drawer front end-up in a vise and use a dovetail square to outline the pins on the end of the board; the wide part of the pins should be on the inside face of the stock. As with the half-blind dovetail (page 120), the spacing is a matter of personal choice, but for a typical drawer, a half-pin at each edge and two evenly spaced pins between provide a good combination of strength and appearance (right). Mark the waste sections with an X as you go. Finally, use a combination square to extend all the dovetail marks down both faces of the board to the shoulder lines.

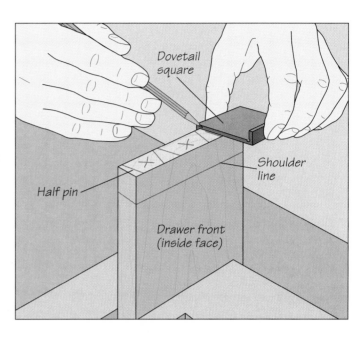

Dovetail square

Shoulder line

Half pin

Drawer front (inside face)

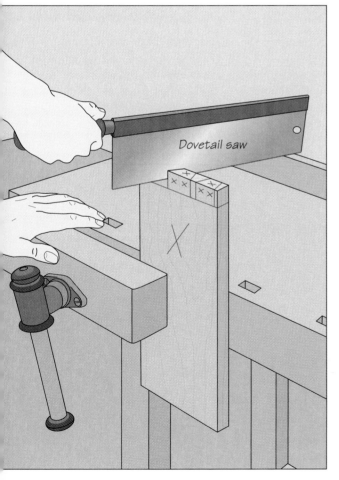

Dovetail saw

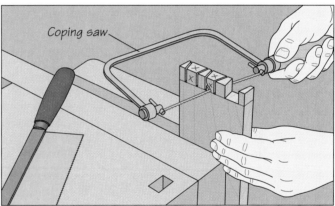

Coping saw

2 Cutting the pins

Leave the drawer front in the vise with its outside face toward you. Use a dovetail saw to cut along the edges of the pins, aligning the saw blade just to the waste side of the cutting line. Cut all the right-hand edges first (left), then complete the left-hand edges. Use smooth, even strokes, taking care to keep the blade level as you cut to the shoulder lines. Once the pins are cut, leave the board in the vise and use a coping saw to remove as much of the waste as possible between the pins. At the side of each pin, slide a coping saw blade into the kerf and rotate the frame without striking the end of the board. Keep the blade about ⅟₁₆ inch above the shoulder line as you cut to the kerf on the edge of the adjacent pin (above). Pare away any remaining waste with a chisel as you would for half-blind dovetails (page 122). Repeat the process at the other end of the drawer front and for the back of the drawer, then mark and cut out the tails on the drawer sides.

DOVETAIL JIGS

Hand-cutting dovetail joints for a large number of drawers takes considerable time and practice. Your router, paired with a commercial dovetail jig like one of those shown on this page, provides an efficient alternative. Although router-and-jig cut dovetails may lack the hand-crafted look of sawn and chiseled joints, they are just as strong, fit together as well and, most importantly, can be produced in a fraction of the time. But remember to factor in setup time for the jigs. If you are making only a couple of drawers, hand tools may well be a faster alternative.

Three popular dovetail jigs are shown below. The model on the left features interchangeable templates. Depending on which template is used, the jig enables a router to cut the pins and tails for half-blind, through dovetails, or box joints with a single setup. The jig in the center consists of two fixed templates for cutting through dovetails. The templates are fastened to backup boards that support the workpiece. One template is used for cutting the pins, the other for the tails. The jig on the right can be used for routing both half-blind and through dovetail joints. Its single adjustable template allows you to vary the size and spacing of the pins

and tails, giving the joints more of a hand-crafted look.

All three jigs work on essentially the same principle. A router is fitted with a dovetail bit and a guide bushing—both usually provided with the jig. By feeding the tool along the template, the bit is guided in and out of the slots to cut away the waste. The fixed-template jig is shown in action above. Once the templates have been attached to backup boards, the pin and tail boards are secured in place. For several identical joints, a stop block can be clamped to the backup boards for repeat cuts. The jig is shown producing the tails of a joint.

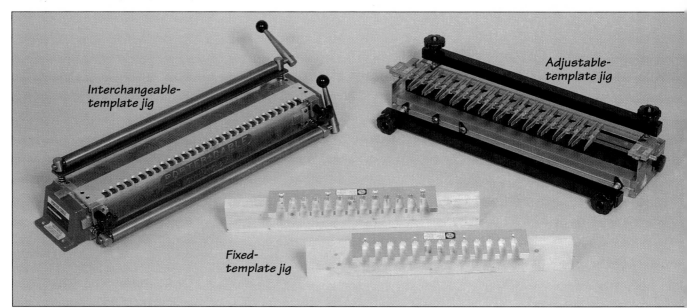

Interchangeable-template jig

Adjustable-template jig

Fixed-template jig

DOUBLE DADO JOINTS

1 Cutting dadoes in a drawer front

Mark one end of the board, dividing its thickness into thirds. Then, install a dado head on your table saw, adjusting the width to one-third the thickness of the drawer front. Set the cutting height equal to the thickness of the drawer sides. Next, install a commercial tenoning jig; the model shown slides in the miter slot. Protecting the stock with a wood pad, clamp the drawer front to the jig. Move the jig sideways to align the marks so that the blades cut the dado in the middle third of the board. Slide the jig along to feed the stock. Turn the drawer front over and clamp it to the jig to cut the dado at the other end *(right)*.

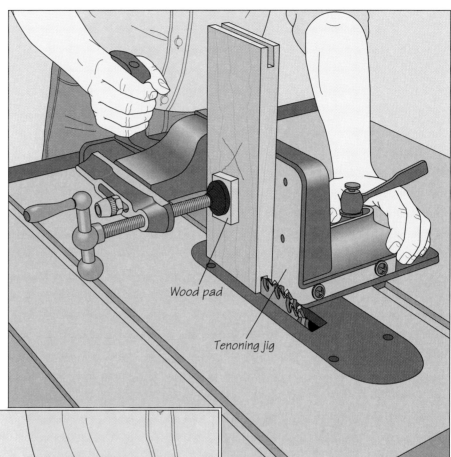

Wood pad

Tenoning jig

Auxiliary fence

Relief notch

Half-tongue

Drawer front

2 Trimming the dado tongues

Install a wooden auxiliary fence on the rip fence, then mark a cutting line on the edge of the drawer front that divides one of the tongues on its inside face in half. With the stock flush against the miter gauge, inside face down, align your mark with the dado head. Butt the fence against the stock and raise the blades to cut a relief notch in the fence. Set the cutting height to trim the half-tongue. Holding the drawer front firmly against the gauge, feed it into the dado head. Turn the board around and repeat the procedure at the other end *(left)*.

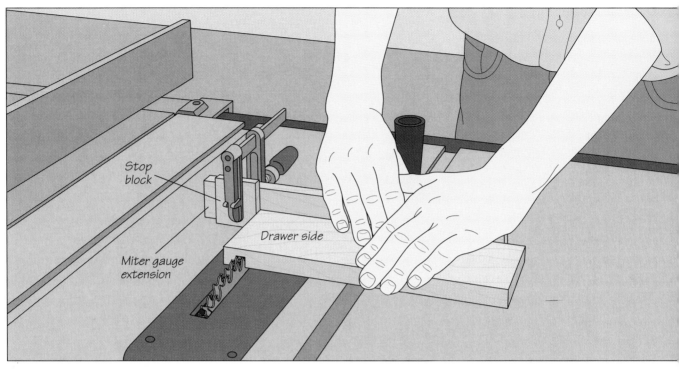

Stop
block

Miter gauge
extension

Drawer side

3 Cutting matching dadoes in the drawer sides

To join the drawer sides to the front, cut a dado near the front end of each side. The dado must mate with the half-tongue on the front. Set the cutting height to the length of the half-tongue and screw a wooden extension board to the miter gauge. To set the width of cut, butt the drawer side against the front and use a pencil to outline the half-tongue on the drawer side. Hold the side against the extension and align the marks with the dado head. Clamp a stop block flush against the end of the stock and feed the board to cut the dado *(above)*. Repeat the cut on the other side.

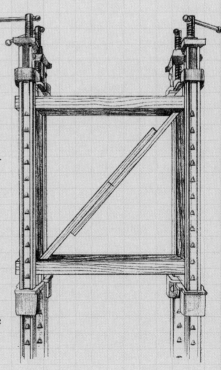

SHOP TIP

Checking drawers for square
To keep drawers square during glue up, measure the diagonals between opposite corners immediately after tightening the clamps. Use two sticks as a measuring jig. Bevel one end of each stick so that it can extend into an inside corner of the drawer. To use the jig, hold the sticks face to face, seat the beveled ends in opposite corners, and mark a line across their edges. Repeat with the two other corners. The two marks should align exactly. If not, the drawer is out-of-square. Correct the problem by loosening the clamps, sliding one jaw of each clamp away from the joint at opposite corners, and retightening.

LIPPED RABBET JOINTS

Cutting a lipped rabbet in a drawer front
To cut lipped rabbets around the edges of a drawer front, mark lines on its inside face to allow for an overhang of at least ⅜ inch *(inset)*. Also mark the rabbet depth on its edges—up to one-half the thickness of the drawer front. Cut the rabbets on the table saw in two steps, first notching the inside face of the front with the blade height set to the depth of the rabbets. These cuts are made with the stock face down on the saw table. Then feed the stock into the blade on end and on edge. Set the blade height to the width of the rabbets, align the blade with the marks for the rabbet depth, and butt the fence against the stock. Keeping the drawer front flush against the fence, feed it on end into the blade to complete one rabbet. Turn the board over and repeat to cut the rabbet at the other end *(right)*. Then feed the stock into the blade on edge to cut the rabbets on the top and bottom edges.

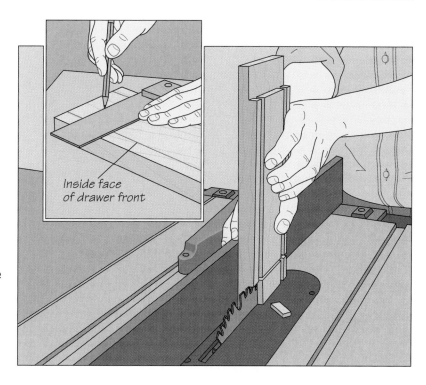

Inside face of drawer front

GLUING UP A DRAWER WITH DADOES OR RABBETS

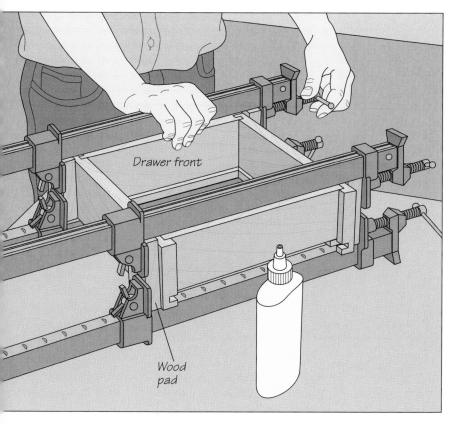

Drawer front

Wood pad

Using bar clamps
Before gluing up a drawer, decide how you will install it *(page 133)*, since side-mounting may require you to prepare the drawer sides before final assembly. Apply glue on all the contacting surfaces of the joints and assemble the drawer. Arrange two bar clamps on a work surface and lay the drawer on them, aligning the bars of the clamps with the drawer front and back. Install two more clamps along the top of the drawer. If you used rabbet joints to assemble the drawer, install another two clamps along the drawer sides. Protect surfaces by placing wood pads between the stock and the clamp jaws. Tighten the clamps just enough to close the joints fully *(left)*, then check the drawer for square *(page 128)*. Finish tightening the clamps until a bead of glue squeezes out of the joints, checking as you go that the corners are square. Once the adhesive has dried, scrape away any dried glue. Slide the bottom panel into place and secure it with finishing nails driven up into the drawer back.

INSTALLING A BOTTOM WITH DRAWER SLIPS

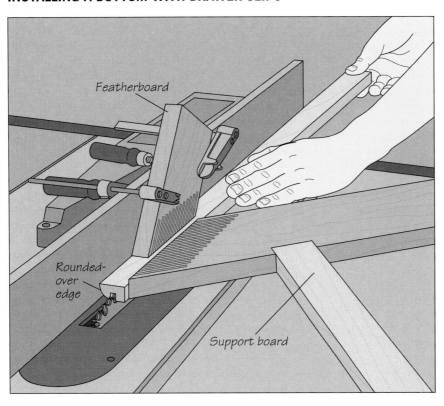

Featherboard

Rounded-
over
edge

Support board

1 Making the slips
For drawer sides made from stock that is too thin to be grooved for a bottom panel, install drawer slips. Slips also provide greater bearing surface for bottom-run drawers. Before the drawer is assembled, prepare your slip stock from a strip of wood—1-by-1 stock is appropriate for most drawers—at least as long as the combined length of the drawer sides. Round over one corner of the board, then set up your table saw to cut a groove in it. Install a dado head, adjusting its width to the thickness of the bottom you will use, and set the cutting height to about ⅜ inch. Position the slip stock flush against the bottom edge of the drawer front and mark the location of the groove on the board. Align the mark with the dado head and position the rip fence against the stock. Clamp on two featherboards, as shown, to support the workpiece. Saw the groove, then crosscut it into two lengths equal to the drawer sides measured from the drawer front.

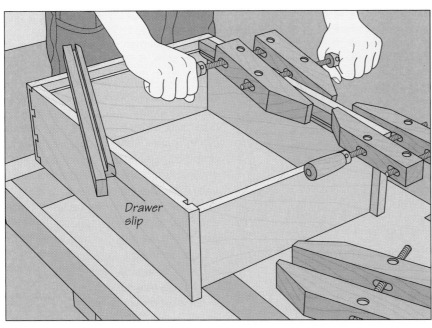

Drawer
slip

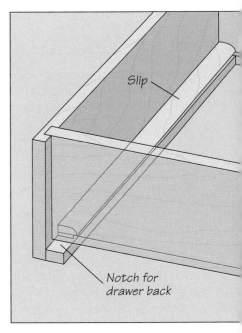

Slip

Notch for
drawer back

2 Mounting the slips on the drawer
Notch the slips so that they clear the back, then set the glued-up drawer upside down on a work surface, spread some glue on the contacting surfaces of the slips, and clamp them against the sides and drawer front (*above, left*). Make certain that the grooves in the slips and drawer front are perfectly aligned (*above, right*).

DRAWER HARDWARE

The faceplate being attached to the drawer front shown at right forms part of a half-mortise lock. The lock bolt extends into a mortise cut in the rail or casework directly above the drawer.

INSTALLING A HALF-MORTISE LOCK

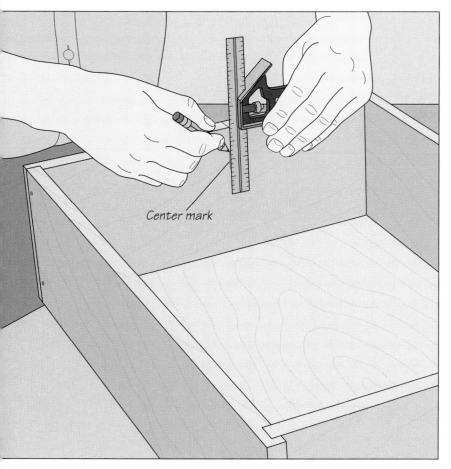

Center mark

1 Centering the lock
Set the drawer on a work surface and mark the midpoint between the sides on the top edge of the front. Then use a combination square to extend the mark onto the inside face of the front *(left)*. Next, hold the lock faceplate *(see photo above)* against the inside of the drawer front, aligning the keyhole with the center mark and keeping the faceplate lip flush with the top edge of the drawer front. Use a pencil to outline the faceplate on the inside face and top edge of the front.

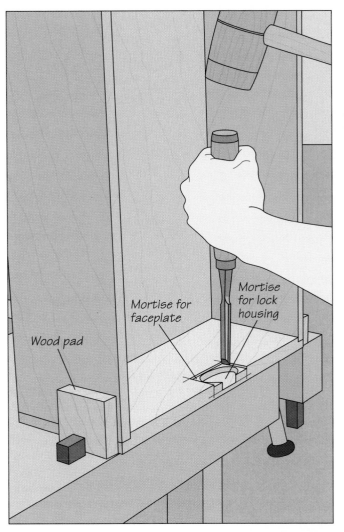

Wood pad

Mortise for faceplate

Mortise for lock housing

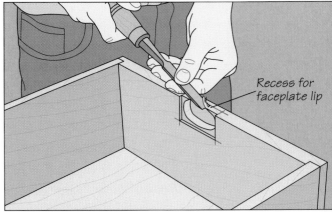

Recess for faceplate lip

2 Cutting the lock mortise

You need to cut three mortises for the lock: one for the face plate, another for the lock housing, and a third for the faceplate lip. This is one of the rare cases when the router is used free-hand. Install a straight bit in the tool, set the cutting depth to the thickness of the faceplate, and cut a mortise inside the marked outline for the faceplate. Start by guiding the tool in a clockwise direction to cut the outside edges of the mortise; clear out the remaining waste by feeding the tool against the direction of bit rotation. Use a chisel to square the corners and pare to the line. For the lock housing, measure the distance between the edges of the faceplate and housing and transfer the measurement to the first mortise. Adjust the router's cutting depth to the thickness of the housing and cut its mortise. Next, use the chisel to cut the recess in the top edge of the drawer front for the faceplate lip *(above)*. Test the fit of the lock in the cavity and use the chisel to deepen or widen any of the mortises, if necessary *(left)*.

3 Cutting the keyhole

Set the lock in the mortise and mark the location of the keyhole. You need to drill two holes for the key: one for the shaft and a smaller hole for the key bit below it. Bore the wider hole first with a bit slightly larger than the key shaft. Then use a bit slightly larger than the thickness of the key bit to bore the second hole. Use a coping saw to join the two holes *(right)*. To finish installing the lock, mount an escutcheon on the outside face of the drawer to protect the wood surrounding the keyhole.

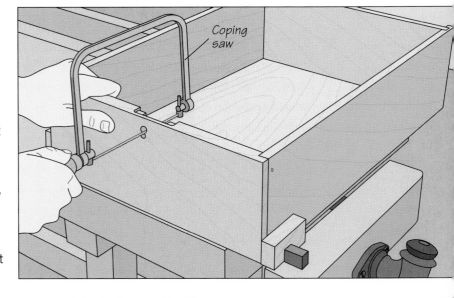

Coping saw

MOUNTING DRAWERS

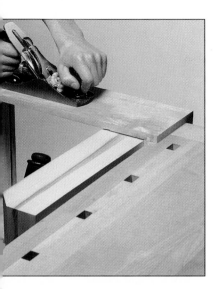

Even careful measurement does not always guarantee a perfect fit. If a drawer is too snug in its opening, you can plane down the sides until the unit opens and closes smoothly.

There are several ways to install drawers in a desk or table. The method you choose should suit the design of your piece and the loads you expect the drawers to bear.

The simplest way to mount a drawer is with side runners. Shown below and on the next pages, this method involves routing grooves in the drawer sides before assembly. These mate with slides mounted on the inside of the casework. Side-mounting is ideal in frame-and-panel casework *(page 135)* and for small- to medium-sized drawers that will bear moderate loads.

Commercial slide runners are another method of side-mounting drawers in a carcase. Although purists may decry their use, commercial runners are stronger than wood runners, and so are a good choice for drawers that will bear heavy loads. Commercial runners are available in different sizes. Buy the hardware and read the manufacturer's instructions before you build your drawers, since runners require specific clearances between the drawer sides and the carcase.

The strongest method of securing drawers is bottom-mounting. Here, the drawers ride on runners mounted in grooves milled in the sides of the casework. The runners are joined at the front and the rear with stretchers, which provide both a bearing surface for the drawers and strengthen the casework. Dust panels *(page 34)* can be added to the frame formed by the runners and stretchers by setting them in a groove routed in their inside edges. Some woodworkers prefer to rout a groove in the carcase sides and install a shelf, which serves double-duty as drawer support and dust panel.

IDE-MOUNTING A DRAWER IN A CARCASE

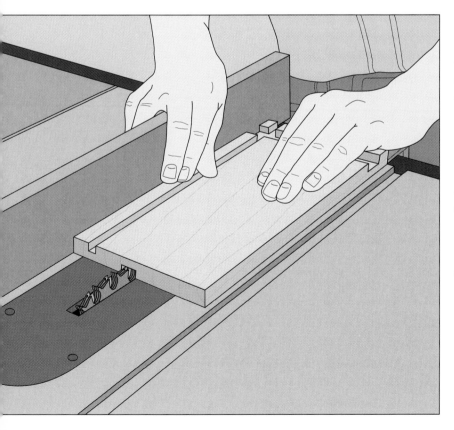

1 Cutting grooves in the drawer sides
Cut a groove in the outside face of each drawer side before final assembly. There are no rigid guidelines for the groove width, but it should accommodate slides that are hefty enough to support the drawer. On your table saw, install a dado head the same width as the groove. Draw cutting lines for the groove width in the middle of the leading end of one drawer side. Set the cutting height at no more than one-half the stock thickness. Butt the lines for the groove width against the dado head, position the rip fence flush against the stock, and make the cut *(left)*. If the groove width exceeds the width of the dado head, turn the board end for end and make another pass. Repeat to cut the groove in the other drawer side.

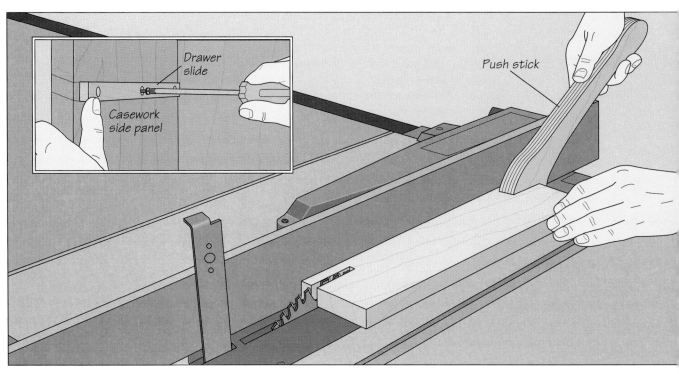

Drawer slide

Casework side panel

Push stick

2 Making and installing the drawer slides

On your table saw, rip the drawer slides from a board that is slightly shorter than the depth of the carcase. Position the rip fence to a cutting width slightly narrower than the grooves in the drawer sides *(step 1)*. Cut two slides for each drawer, using a push stick *(above)*. **(Caution: Blade guard removed for clarity.)** To mount the slides, insert the drawer in the carcase and hold it in place while using a pencil to mark the location of the grooves on the front edges of the side panels. Then use a carpenter's square to extend the marks across the inside faces of the panels. Bore three countersunk clearance holes through the slides; make the clearance holes slightly wider than the screw shanks to allow for wood movement. Holding the slides recessed from the front edge of the carcase between the marked lines on the side panels, drill pilot holes and screw the slides in place *(inset)*. Test-fit the drawer. Use shims under the slides to tighten it or deepen the grooves to ease the fit.

SHOP TIP

Positioning drawer slides
To ensure drawer slides on opposite sides of your carcase are at precisely the same height, use a wood spacer cut from a piece of scrap. Make its width equal to the necessary space between the slides. Hold the edge of the spacer against the top and the face against one side panel, butt the slide against the spacer, and screw it in place. Repeat the procedure for the remaining slides.

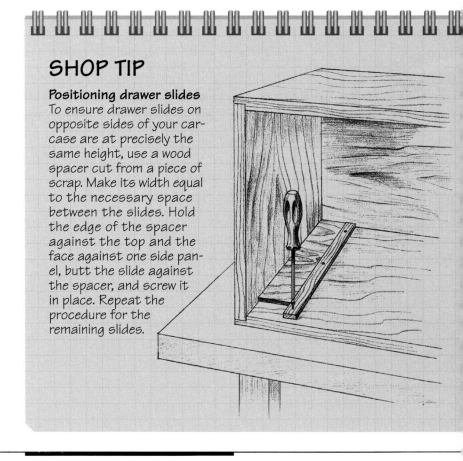

DRAWERS IN FRAME-AND-PANEL CASEWORK

Installing drawers in frame-and-panel casework is a little more complicated than with carcases. Runners cannot be used because drawer supports cannot be fastened directly to the floating panels. As shown at right and on page 136, the supports are instead attached to corner strips screwed to the stiles of the casework. The drawer supports are fixed in the dadoes. During installation, hold the corner strips in position with handscrews and test-fit the drawers to make sure the supports hold them straight and level. The strips can run the full height of the casework to support several drawers, or be shortened to mount a single drawer in a piece of furniture like the night table shown at right.

SIDE-MOUNTING A DRAWER IN A FRAME-AND-PANEL CASE

Screw head

1 Making the corner strips
Rip a board to a width of 4 inches and crosscut it to reach from top to bottom inside the case. The dadoes for the drawer supports are easy to cut on a radial arm saw. Install a dado head, adjusting its width to accommodate the thickness of the supports you will use in step 3. Starting at the end that will be at the bottom of the cabinet, cut a dado for the lowest drawer. Slide the board along the fence to cut the second dado at the next drawer position. If the distance between the supports will be equal, drive a screw into the fence to serve as an indexing pin; locate the head of the fastener against the left edge of the first dado. Now cut the second dado and reposition the board so the left edge of this dado rests against the screw head. Cut the remaining dadoes in this fashion *(left)*, then rip the board into four equal strips.

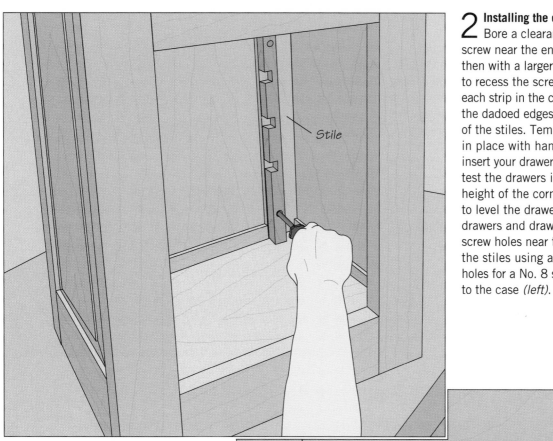

Stile

2 Installing the corner strips
Bore a clearance hole for a No. 8 screw near the end of each corner strip, then with a larger bit, drill deep enough to recess the screw head. Now position each strip in the case, making certain that the dadoed edges are flush with the edge of the stiles. Temporarily hold the strips in place with handscrews, make and insert your drawer supports *(step 3)*, and test the drawers in the case. Adjust the height of the corner strips, if necessary, to level the drawers. Then remove the drawers and drawer supports, mark the screw holes near the top and bottom of the stiles using an awl, and bore pilot holes for a No. 8 screw. Screw the strips to the case *(left)*.

Drawer support

Corner strip

3 Inserting the drawer supports
Measure the distance between the front and back stiles on both sides of the case. Cut drawer supports to fit the gaps between matching pairs of dadoes. Make sure that the supports are wide enough to buttress the drawers adequately, and that they fit snugly in the dadoes *(right)*.

FINE-TUNING A DRAWER TO FIT

Planing drawer sides

If a drawer binds in a piece of furniture, you can use a hand plane to improve the fit. If the sides bind, remove the drawer and find and mark any shiny areas on the sides—these are high spots that can be shaved with the plane. Secure the drawer on a work surface so the binding side is facing up. Gripping the plane with both hands, shave off the marked spots with smooth, even strokes *(right)*. Test-fit the drawer in its opening and continue planing until it fits perfectly.

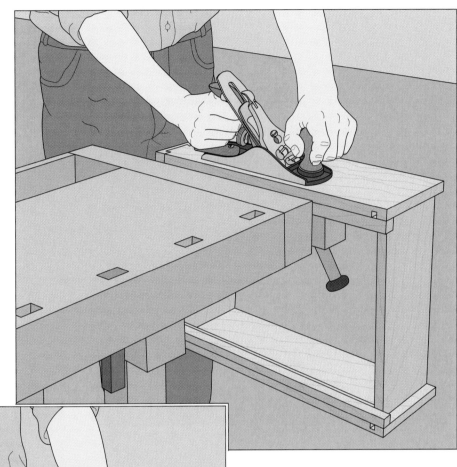

Planing the top of a drawer

If the top or bottom of the drawer rubs against part of the casework, plane the top. To hold the drawer in place, secure one side between bench dogs, using wood pads to protect the stock. Plane the edge to be trimmed with a light, even pass *(left)*. Test-fit and continue planing, as necessary.

DRAWER STOPS

Drawer stops control how far a drawer can slide in or out. Inward stops are almost always needed. They prevent a drawer from being pushed in too far.

Outward stops, to prevent a drawer from pulling out of a carcase, are always needed when a drawer carries a heavy load, and may be desirable at other times as well. The following pages show a few methods for installing both types of stops.

The inward stop shown at left will allow the front of the drawer to rest exactly flush with the carcase front. It is installed on the dust panel supporting the drawer, offset from the front edge by the thickness of the drawer front. To make this method work, the drawer front must overhang the bottom so the inside face of the front contacts the stop when the drawer is closed.

INWARD STOPS

Attaching an eccentric stop

This is an easy-to-install adjustable stop. Before installing the back panel of your carcase, use a band saw or saber saw to cut a 1- to 1½-inch-diameter disk from a piece of scrap wood the same thickness as the drawer sides. Bore an off-center hole through the stop, then screw the disk to the side panel near the back. Set the case on its side and close the drawer. Loosen the screw slightly and rotate the stop until it just touches the drawer, then tighten the screw *(right).*

OUTWARD STOPS: CARCASE

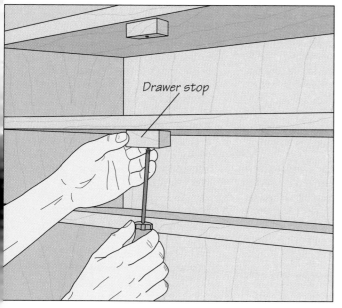

Drawer stop

Installing an outward drawer stop
Cut a stop from a piece of scrap wood. Before gluing up the drawer, cut a notch for the stop in the drawer back. Make the notch deeper than the stop's thickness and wider than its narrow dimension to allow the stop to fit through the opening when you install the drawer. For the desk pedestal shown above, the stop is fixed to the underside of the shelf or dust panel. To mount the stop, install the drawer and mark the location of the notch on the frame above the drawer. Bore a pilot hole through the stop, then screw it in position *(above, left)*. Do not tighten the screw all the way. With the long edge of the stop parallel to the sides of the case, slip the drawer in place *(above, right)*. Once the stop passes completely through the notch, rotate it 90° so that its long edge is parallel to the drawer back and tighten the screw.

OUTWARD STOPS: FRAME-AND-PANEL

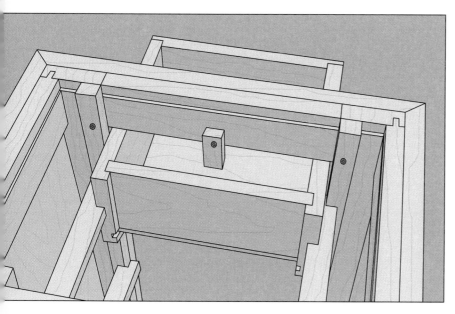

Installing a stop on the front rail
This method works for the top drawer of a frame-and-panel desk or one with drawer rails between each drawer. Cut a drawer stop from scrap. To mount the stop, bore a pilot hole near one end. Screw the stop to the middle of the rail, leaving the fastener just loose enough so that you can rotate the stop out of the way. Install the drawer. Once the drawer back clears the front rail, rotate the stop 90° *(left)*.

GLOSSARY

A-B-C

Base molding: A decorative frame made from molded stock that supports the bottom of a desk.

Bound water: Moisture held within the cell walls of wood; see *free water*.

Breadboard end: A narrow strip of wood installed across the end grain of a tabletop to conceal that grain.

Cabriole leg: A type of furniture leg characterized by rounded contours designed to imitate the graceful leg of a leaping animal.

Carcase: A piece of furniture with a box-like construction; made from solid panels.

Casework: The framework of a piece of furniture constructed either from solid panels or from frame-and-panel assemblies.

Cope-and-stick joint: A method of joining stiles and rails in frame-and-panel construction; the joint features mating tongues and grooves and a decorative molding.

Crosscut: A saw cut made across the grain of a workpiece.

D-E-F-G-H-I

Dado: A rectangular channel cut into a workpiece.

Desktop fastener: Metal hardware that fastens the leg-and-rail assembly of a table or desk to the top; installed in shallow recesses cut into the mating pieces.

Dividing extension table: An extension table with a tabletop and leg-and-rail assembly that slide apart to accommodate additional leaves; see *non-dividing extension table*.

Double dado joint: A corner joint that features a tongue in each piece that interlocks with a groove in the other.

Dovetailed half-lap joint: Used for joining the connecting rail of a desk to the carcase; the half-lap at the end of the rail is cut in a dovetail shape to lock the joint in tension.

Dowel joint: Any joint relying on dowels for alignment or reinforcement.

Drawer slide: A type of drawer support; usually a wood strip fastened to the side panel of a carcase that mates with a groove in the drawer side, or a commercial metal slide fastened to the drawer side that meshes with a runner screwed to the carcase.

Drawer slip: A grooved wood strip fastened along the bottom edge of a drawer side to support the bottom.

Drawer stop: A wooden block or disk attached to desk or table casework to prevent a drawer from being pulled out or pushed in too far.

Drop-leaf table: A table with a narrow top and hinged leaves that fold down when not in use.

Dust frame: A flat frame-and-panel assembly used to support desk drawers and prevent dust from entering the drawers.

Escutcheon: A metal plate installed around a keyhole for decoration and protection of the surrounding wood.

Extension table: A table with a top that opens on table extenders to accommodate additional spacer leaves. See *dividing* and *non-dividing extension tables*.

False front: A piece of wood installed over a drawer front, usually to conceal the end grain of the sides or to create a lipped front.

Fiber saturation point (FSP): A condition in which wood cell cavities are free of all water, while the cell walls remain fully saturated.

Flush front: A drawer front that sits flush with the front edges of the carcase when the drawer is installed; also known as an inset drawer.

Frame-and-panel assembly: A method of casework construction in which a wood panel sits in grooves in a frame made of horizontal rails and vertical stiles.

Free water: Moisture contained within wood cell cavities; see *bound water*.

Gateleg table: A six-legged table with two legs that swing out from the table rails to support drop leaves.

Grain: The arrangement and direction of the fibers that make up wood; grain appearance varies with the wood species and the sawing technique.

Half-blind dovetail joint: Similar to a through dovetail joint, except that the pins are not cut through the entire thickness of the workpiece, thereby concealing the end grain of the tail boards; ideal for joining drawer fronts to sides.

Haunched mortise-and-tenon joint: Similar to a standard mortise-and-tenon joint, except that one edge of the tenon has a haunch that fills the groove cut for a panel.

Inlay: A decorative strip of metal, wood, or marquetry that is glued into a groove cut into a workpiece.

J-K-L-M-N-O-P-Q

Lap joint: A joint in which one or both of the mating boards are dadoed so that the surfaces of the pieces rest flush with one another when the joint is assembled.

edger strip: A short, narrow piece of wood used to support the top or bottom of a table or desk.

ipped front: A rabbeted drawer front that overhangs the sides, concealing drawer-mounting hardware when the drawer is closed; also serves as a drawer stop.

Marquetry: Decorative inlay done with veneers, metal, or other materials.

Mortise-and-tenon joint: A joinery technique in which a projecting tenon cut in one board fits into a matching hole, or mortise, in another.

Nominal size: The dimensions to which lumber is sawn before planing; wood is sold according to nominal size.

Non-dividing extension table: An extension table with top slides that open on table extenders while the leg-and-rail assembly remains fixed; see *dividing extension table*.

Outward stop: A wood block that stops a drop-leaf support in the open position; also, a block screwed to the inside of a carcase to prevent a drawer from being pulled out too far.

Pedestal table: A table with a top that is supported by a central column usually mounted on three or four short legs.

Plain-sawn lumber: Lumber that has been sawn so that the wide surfaces are roughly parallel to the annual growth rings. Also known as flat-sawn lumber when referring to softwood; see *quartersawn lumber*.

Pocket hole: An angled hole bored into the face of a workpiece and exiting from its top edge; typically used to attach a top to the rails of a table or desk.

Pommel: The square section left on a turned furniture leg; allows room for mortises needed to receive rails.

Quartersawn lumber: Wood sawn so the wide surfaces intersect the growth rings at angles between 45° to 90°. Also known as vertical-grained lumber when referring to softwood; see *plain-sawn lumber*.

R-S

Rabbet: A step-like cut in the edge or end of a board; usually forms part of a joint.

Rabbet joint: A method of joining wood in which the end or edge of one workpiece fits into a channel cut along the edge or end of another workpiece; typically used to join carcases at the corners.

Rail: A board running along the bottom edge of a tabletop to which the legs can be attached; also, the horizontal member of a frame-and-panel assembly. See *stile*.

Raised panel: In frame-and-panel construction, a carcase panel with a bevel cut around its edges, a decorative effect that "raises" the center and allows the panel to fit into the groove cut in the frame.

Relative humidity: The ratio of the water vapor present in the air to the amount the air would hold at its saturation point, usually expressed as a percentage figure.

Rip cut: A saw cut that follows the grain of a workpiece.

Rule joint: A pivoting joint commonly used in drop-leaf tables; features mating concave and convex profiles cut into edges of the table leaf and tabletop.

Seasoning: The process or technique of removing moisture from green wood to improve its workability.

Stile: The vertical member of a frame-and-panel assembly. See *rail*.

Substrate: A piece of plywood or solid wood used as the foundation for veneer, leather, felt, or tile that covers the surface of a table or desk top.

Swing-leg table: A four-legged table with two legs that swing out from the rails to support drop leaves.

T-U-V-W-X-Y-Z

Tabletop evener: Hardware installed on the underside of adjustable tables to align the table halves or leaves as they are closed.

Tangential plane: A viewing plane in wood identification cut along the grain tangential to the growth rings; plain-sawn lumber is sawn tangentially.

Template: A pattern cut from plywood, hardwood, or particleboard to reproduce multiple copies of a part.

Through dovetail joint: A method of joining wood at the corners by means of interlocking pins and tails, both cut to the thickness of the workpiece.

Trestle table: A knockdown table with a large top supported by trestles at each end that are connected to rails with removable wedged or tusk tenon joints.

Tripod table: A pedestal table with a central column supported by three shorter legs.

Tusk tenon joint: A type of through mortise-and-tenon joint in which the tenon extends through the mortise piece and is fixed, not by glue, but by a tusk-like wedge.

Wood movement: The shrinking or swelling of wood in reaction to changes in relative humidity.

INDEX

Page references in *italics* indicate an illustration of subject matter. Page references in **bold** indicate a Build It Yourself project.

ACKNOWLEDGMENTS

The editors wish to thank the following:

TABLE AND DESK BASICS
Judith Ames, Seattle, WA; Delta International Machinery/Porter-Cable, Guelph, Ont.;
Hitachi Power Tools U.S.A. Ltd., Norcross, GA; Hank Holtzer, Seattle, WA;
Thomas Moser Cabinetmakers, Auburn, ME; Shopsmith, Inc., Montreal, Que.

DESK CASEWORK
Adjustable Clamp Co., Chicago, IL; Black & Decker/Elu Power Tools, Towson, MD; Delta International
Machinery/Porter-Cable, Guelph, Ont.; Freud Westmore Tools, Ltd., Mississauga, Ont.;
Great Neck Saw Mfrs. Inc. (Buck Bros. Division), Millbury, MA; Griset Industries, Inc., Santa Ana, CA;
Frank Klausz, Frank's Cabinet Shop, Pluckemin, NJ; Sandvik Saws and Tools Co., Scranton, PA;
Stanley Tools, Division of the Stanley Works, New Britain, CT; Steiner-Lamello A.G. Switzerland/Colonial
Saw Co., Kingston, MA; Vermont American Corp., Lincolnton, NC and Louisville, KY;
The Woodworker's Store, Rogers, MN

LEGS AND RAILS
Adjustable Clamp Co., Chicago, IL; American Tool Cos., Lincoln, NE; Black & Decker/Elu Power Tools,
Towson, MD; Delta International Machinery/Porter-Cable, Guelph, Ont.; Allan Flegg, Montreal, Que.;
Lee Valley Tools Ltd., Ottawa, Ont.; Robert Sorby Ltd., Sheffield, U.K./Busy Bee Machine Tools,
Concord, Ont.; Sandvik Saws and Tools Co., Scranton, PA; Sears, Roebuck and Co., Chicago, IL;
Vermont American Corp., Lincolnton, NC and Louisville, KY; Wainbee Ltd., Pointe Claire, Que./
De-Sta-Co, Troy, MI; The Woodworker's Store, Rogers, MN

TOPS
American Tool Cos., Lincoln, NE; Black & Decker/Elu Power Tools, Towson, MD; Cabot Safety Corp.,
Southbridge, MA; Delta International Machinery/Porter-Cable, Guelph, Ont.; Allan Flegg, Montreal, Que.;
Freud Westmore Tools, Ltd., Mississauga, Ont.; Great Neck Saw Mfrs. Inc. (Buck Bros. Division),
Millbury, MA; Lee Valley Tools Ltd., Ottawa, Ont.; Edna and William Mills, Montreal, Que.;
Sears, Roebuck and Co., Chicago, IL; Stanley Tools, Division of the Stanley Works, New Britain, CT;
Steiner-Lamello A.G. Switzerland/Colonial Saw Co., Kingston, MA; 3M Canada Inc., London, Ont.;
Vermont American Corp., Lincolnton, NC and Louisville, KY; The Woodworker's Store, Rogers, MN

DRAWERS
Adjustable Clamp Co., Chicago, IL; American Tool Cos., Lincoln, NE; Delta International
Machinery/Porter-Cable, Guelph, Ont.; Freud Westmore Tools, Ltd., Mississauga, Ont.; Great Neck Saw
Mfrs. Inc. (Buck Bros. Division), Millbury, MA; Frank Klausz, Frank's Cabinet Shop, Pluckemin, NJ;
Robert Larson Company, Inc., San Francisco, CA; Leigh Industries Inc., Port Coquitlam, B.C.;
Record Tools Inc., Pickering, Ont.; Sandvik Saws and Tools Co., Scranton, PA;
Sears, Roebuck and Co., Chicago, IL; Stanley Tools, Division of the Stanley Works, New Britain, CT;
Vermont American Corp., Lincolnton, NC and Louisville, KY; The Woodworker's Store, Rogers, MN

The following persons also assisted in the preparation of this book:

Eric Cordeau (Les Bois D'Ecor, Montreal, Que.), Lorraine Doré,
Mr. and Mrs. Richard Ettinger, Graphor Consultation, Geneviève Monette, David Simon

PICTURE CREDITS

Cover Robert Chartier
6, 7 Robert Holmes
8, 9 Ian Gittler
10, 11 Michael Tincher
13 Philip C. Jackson
22 Courtesy Thos. Moser Cabinetmakers
25 Hank Holtzer
27 Judith Ames
90 Dean Powell/Kam Ghaffari Design